Light Your Path

Timeless Wisdom for Young People

Pathways for Healthy Mind, Body, and Spirit

Chris Ellis

Dedication

This book is dedicated to Hogan and Keyvan

Both of you were with me every moment of this journey.
I love you more than the stars in the sky.

Acknowledgments

The author would like to thank the following people for their wisdom, support, and love:

Lisa Ellis, Thomas Ellis, Alice Ellis, Shane Eady
Yasha Horstman, Richard Burbach, Chris Burke, Andy Novak,
Sandy Anderson, and Thomas Winninger

Table of **Contents**

Introduction

This book is a guide for exploring who you are, who you can become, and what goes into living a healthy and joyful life during a time of much personal growth. Your life is a great journey with many ups and downs and highs and lows along the way. The only thing for certain, in an uncertain world, is that it will be an amazing adventure.

The book is an introduction to the wisdom of sound mind, body, and spirit. Wisdom can be defined as the use of awareness, experience, and insight to help ensure the wellbeing of yourself and others. Considered by many as the greatest virtue, wisdom is the light of understanding that shines most bright when you walk your path with an open heart.

The book draws on thousands of years of wisdom teachings from the world's great traditions, cultures, religions, and schools of thought. Open your heart and mind to some of history's great teachers, clerics, artists, mystics, scholars, leaders, and sages. Find out more about these exceptional people. Discover how fascinating their journeys have been.

The book is designed to be read from start to end. There is a subtle flow to the text. But you don't have to read it in order. You can use it any way you wish. You can pick a page or two each day or each week at random. Or find a topic you are interested in and start there. In a quiet place, read it carefully by yourself or with a friend or a group.

Take your time reading this book. Think about what it is saying to you. Use it to have conversations with family members, friends, and teachers about the qualities of good character and what it means to be a luminous young person in an exciting universe. Challenge yourself and others. Enjoy and embrace the many secrets found within.

Table of Modules

Each page has one or more of these twelve recurring modules:

Light your path. Timeless values and virtues for daily living.

Have you heard? Quotes from eminent people through the ages.

Shine the light. Principles related to healthy mind-body-spirit.

True nature is. Exercises in relating to authentic beingness.

Did you know? Inspiring and challenging wisdom teachings.

Check your reality. Explorations in perception and experience.

Around the world. Views from diverse traditions and cultures.

Do you understand? Mind-bending stories, parables, and proverbs.

Think about this. Mini-lessons in awareness and mindfulness.

Change your mind. Ideas for changing perspective and mindset.

Haiku for you. Short poems about nature and consciousness.

Epigram I am. Twists of logic with thought-provoking humor.

Did you know?

Your path is the great source of wisdom.

Your path is created by fully experiencing life each day.

Your path is an awakening to your true self in a changing world.

And did you know?

Through the ages, wise ones agreed on many of the secrets to life.

Often called wisdom teachings, they aren't really secrets.

They will help you walk your path with joy.

Are you ready to explore these "secrets" and fully experience your amazing journey?

Pathways

Part 1

Topics

Honesty ~ Curiosity ~ Open-mindedness

Compassion ~ Giving and receiving ~ Ethics and morality

Courage ~ Humility ~ Friendship ~ Equality

Loving-kindness ~ Heart-centeredness

Light your path

Light your path with **Honesty**. How do *you* define honesty? How do you show it? Blaze a trail this way…

I tell the truth. I tell the truth even when it might be inconvenient. I am careful to not intentionally hurt someone with the truth. I am honest and kind at the same time. I say what I mean and do what I say. I act with integrity. I keep my word. When I say *yes* or *no* to something, I follow through on my commitment. I take responsibility for my actions and admit when I do the wrong thing or make a mistake. I do not try to be someone I am not. I avoid fibs and excuses. I avoid exaggerating and spreading rumors. I don't leave out important information on purpose. I choose what is right over what is easy. I am trustworthy.

Pathways to **honesty** come from a power within you. For example, if you are no longer interested in someone as your boyfriend or girlfriend, you tell the truth as soon as you make this decision. You do not hurt his or her feelings on purpose, but you don't make-up false reasons for ending the relationship. You simply are clear that your feelings have changed. There is nothing wrong with this! It is human for feelings to change. You know that because you care for a person, telling the truth in a careful manner is better for you and him or her in the long run.

Today, try to observe and reflect on all the different ways in which you are honest or dishonest.

Have you heard?

"Proclaim the truth and do not be silent through fear." Catherine of Siena ~Sainted Italian Christian theologian and philosopher

"Truth does not change because it is, or is not, believed." Hypatia ~Greek-Alexandrian astronomer, scholar, librarian, and teacher

What do you think they meant? Why are honesty and integrity so important in your life?

Shine the light

Honest inquiry is the combination of both honesty and curiosity.

When asking questions, consider these principles: Be honest about what you know and do not know. Ask questions that are genuine and not opinions in disguise. Be sincere about wanting to learn from others.

Healthy inquiry counteracts the dangers of certainty and conformity.

Consider asking these types of open-ended questions: What forces are shaping how we live and why? How do things work and how can they be improved? What is happening in your community? What do you wish were different and why? What are the qualities of a good life

Exploring questions together requires the integrity of those involved.

Consider trying these practices: Openly discuss issues using solid facts and evidence. Use common sense to find common ground for the common good. Apply sound reason and judgement to pursue progress.

A proverb from ancient Greece, often attributed to Seneca the Stoic philosopher, is helpful: **No one was ever wise by chance.**

How might you start asking questions in a more sincere way? How might you treat each day as an opportunity to learn more about the mystery of life?

Have you heard?

"It isn't what we don't know that gives us trouble, it's what we know that ain't so." Will Rogers ~Cherokee-American actor and humorist

"The ideal subject of totalitarian rule is the person for whom the distinction between fact and fiction, true and false, no longer exists." Hannah Arendt ~Jewish-American philosopher and political theorist

What do you think they meant?

Epigram I am

When I honestly seek the truth,

I never allow facts to interrupt my search!

Light your path

Light your path with **Curiosity**. How do *you* define curiosity? How do you show it? Blaze a trail this way...

I ask a lot of questions. I seek to understand and learn new things. I have a sense for what I do not know and learn as much about the world as I can. I go beyond a shallow understanding of something by doing research, reading books, listening to podcasts, and watching documentaries and video posts. I study things deeply. I pay attention in school and ask thoughtful questions in class. I explore new things and try new experiences. I am open to the opinions of other people and I am willing to be surprised, perhaps even disturbed, since it is an opportunity to grow. I am interested in other people, places, and ideas.

Pathways to **curiosity** come from a power within you. For example, when you find out a friend is from another country, you ask him about his homeland, and in doing so, you show a genuine interest in him, his culture, and his perspective. Or maybe you find out that a friend has a very different life at home than you do, maybe because she has gay parents. So you ask about her experience, but also respect her privacy if she is not interested in sharing.

Today, try to ask open-ended questions in a variety of conversations without giving your opinion.

Have you heard?

"Nothing in life is to be feared; it is only to be understood." Marie Curie ~Polish-French physicist and chemist

"Wonder is the desire for knowledge." Thomas Aquinas ~Sainted Italian Catholic priest and philosopher

What do you think they meant? Why are curiosity and learning so important?

Did you know?

The nature of learning is curiosity.

Curiosity involves learning about nature.

Learning about nature is experiencing nature.

What do these principles mean? How might they help you walk your path?

Have you heard?

"In every walk with nature, one receives far more than he seeks." John Muir ~Scottish-American naturalist and conservationist

"Look deep into nature, and then you will understand." Albert Einstein ~German-American physicist, philosopher, and teacher

What do you think they meant?

True nature is

Look deep into the sea. Study the depths of the oceans and the diversity of life there. Do this by reading books, watching videos, or even snorkeling or scuba-diving yourself someday.

Look deep into the jungles and woodlands. Study the depths of the rainforests. Do this by reading books, watching videos, or visiting them yourself someday. Go for long walks in nature whenever you can.

Look deep into the canyons and river gorges. Study the depths of caves and caverns along the way. Do this by reading books, watching videos, or exploring them yourself someday.

Look deep into cells that make up life and matter. Study the deep mysteries of molecules and atoms and superstrings. Do this by reading books, watching videos, or using a microscope when available.

Look deep into space. Study the stars. Learn how the universe formed. Do this by reading books, watching videos, or using a telescope when you have the opportunity. You might even travel into space someday.

How might you learn more about nature? How might you experience it?

Light your path

Light your path with **Open-mindedness**. How do *you* define it? How do you show it? Blaze a trail this way...

I listen to the views of other people and seek to understand their ideas and beliefs. I am sincere in learning from them, even if I do not agree. I can disagree and still respect what they have to offer. I avoid being overly critical or judgmental. This does not mean that I ignore reason, facts, and evidence. Not all ideas are equal in quality or equally valid. And I avoid believing in things just because I want them to be true. I am open to new ideas and explore new perspectives and ways of doing things. Ignorance is a dark force in the world, and so I am willing to educate myself and help others learn as well.

Pathways to **open-mindedness** come from a power within you. For example, when working on a school project with other classmates, and one of them suggests a new way of doing the project, you listen carefully and respect and consider her recommendation, even though it seems very different from what you suggested. You ask sincere questions and then work as a team to decide the best approach.

Today, try to listen closely to others, be a sponge, and soak-up each new idea you hear with an open mind.

Have you heard?

"In the beginner's mind there are many possibilities, but in the expert's mind there are few." Shunryu Suzuki ~Japanese Zen master, teacher, missionary, and writer

"All knowledge begins with the senses, proceeds to understanding, and ends with reason." Immanuel Kant ~German enlightenment philosopher of idealism and realism

What do you think he meant? Why are both open-mindedness and reason so important?

Haiku for you

The ocean wind, warm sand

My friend talks sincere nonsense

Sun and I listen

Shine the light

Sincere interest **is an openness and willingness to learn with and from others who may have different views.**

Emmet Fox, the spiritual wisdom teacher, once said "No one can be considered truly intelligent who does not have a readiness to examine new ideas with an open mind."

Ideas offered with sincerity should be respected. Ideas don't have to be original or fact-based to be worthwhile.

Readiness means remembering that each of us has something to offer and can contribute to the conversation. We can show a genuine interest in ideas and beliefs that are not our own.

Readiness also means a willingness to really listen. We can listen to others with complete attention, without interrupting, criticizing, or rehearsing what we want to say in response.

A proverb from the Upanishads, an ancient Sanskrit text, suggests this: **Let noble thoughts come to us from all directions.**

We can be aware of our own biases and points of view, and we can take care in how we discuss ideas, ask questions, seek to understand, and not unduly judge or criticize people who offer them.

Objective reason, science, and law are vital to society. Fact-based truth is essential. We can also appreciate subjective beliefs, like spirituality and the supernatural, and discern the difference.

How might you share ideas and explore questions with others in a less-opinionated way?

Change your mind

Use a new mindset to have conversations with people about ideas.

Stop listening with this frame: Is it right? Do I agree?

Start listening with this frame: What does it mean? What can I learn?

Light your path

Light your path with **Compassion**. How do *you* define compassion? How do you show it? Blaze a trail this way...

I am friendly and caring with myself. I care about my own wellbeing and the wellbeing of others. I am kind, especially when someone is struggling. I am generous with my time and resources when able. I notice when others are sick, sad, hurt, or in trouble, and help them whenever I can. I recognize and try to relate to their distress. But I avoid allowing their suffering to transfer to me. I share what I have when others don't have enough. I help protect them when they cannot protect themselves. I show up when a friend is in pain even if all I can do is just be there for them.

Pathways to **compassion** come from a power within you. For example, if there is a girl at school who is very poor, you share your food with her at lunch if she is hungry, if you have enough. And if she is criticized, you tell other kids to stop making fun of the clothes she wears or how she looks or how she acts. Or if there is a boy who is mentally disabled, or handicapped in some way, you defend him from the ridicule of others. Or if a loner in school gets bullied, you never participate and are clear with your friends you will not be involved in that kind of activity in any way. You are dedicated to preventing the bullying of others.

Today, try to help several people in meaningful ways that other people won't even notice.

Have you heard?

"Do unto others as you would have them do unto you." Jesus Christ ~Jewish prophet and spiritual leader of Christianity

"The most precious gift you can offer anyone is your attention." Thich Nhat Hanh ~Vietnamese Buddhist spiritual leader and writer

"If you want others to be happy, practice compassion. If you want to be happy, practice compassion." The Dalai Lama ~Tibetan and Buddhist spiritual leader

What do you think they meant? Why is caring about other people so important?

Did you know?

You cannot get from others what you don't already have.

You cannot keep what you have if you don't give it away.

And did you know?

In caring about others, you care about yourself.

In caring about yourself, you care about others.

What do these principles mean? How might they help you walk your path?

Have you heard?

"The best way to find yourself is to lose yourself in the service of others. Be the change you wish to see in the world." Mahatma Gandhi ~Indian human rights leader and activist

"No one has ever become poor by giving." Anne Frank ~German-born diarist and young victim of the Holocaust

What do you think he meant? Why is it important to take action and help others?

Around the world

Ayni

(pronounced *ai-nee*)

Ayni originates from the Andes mountains of South America, and is used by indigenous people of Peru, Ecuador, and Bolivia. It means to give and receive in a beneficial way and in gratitude.

Ayni is cooperation and reciprocity. It says everything is connected, and the backbone of life in any community is the mutual act of giving and receiving between people and between people and nature.

Do you understand?

There was once a wise woman who lived in an abbey and worked in the abbey's library. The library's most-prized possessions were three ancient scrolls on which were written verses of timeless wisdom.

One day a monk came running to her and screamed, "Sister! Someone has stolen our precious scrolls!" Two scrolls were missing, but the third was on the floor near the door to the outside, dropped by the thief.

The librarian quickly picked up the third scroll and ran outside to catch the thief. After a long chase through the forest, she caught him. He collapsed and surrendered himself, thinking he would be punished.

Instead, she gave him the third scroll and said, "You left the most important one. The others are incomplete without it. It holds the keys to true joy. Here, please take it." She smiled and returned to the abbey.

The thief could not believe what had just happened. He gathered up all three scrolls and followed her back to the abbey where he committed himself to becoming one of its most faithful students.

What does this story mean to you? Why are right and wrong are not always so clear?

Have you heard?

"I tore away from the safe comfort of certainties through my love for the truth." Simone de Beauvoir ~French existentialist philosopher, writer, and feminist

"Out beyond the ideas of wrongdoing and rightdoing, there is a field. I will meet you there." Rumi ~Persian poet and Sufi mystic

What do you think they meant?

Shine the light

For thousands of years we have wondered about ethics, morality, and the nature of right and wrong, good and evil, virtue and vice.

Many people have studied ideal human values and character. Most agree that we behave based on a combination of three things: our beliefs, ability to reason, and self-interest. But there is no single definition of what is right or wrong, ethical or moral.

And each of us has a shadow self of weakness, desire, and fear, the dark areas of our psyche. So there is much debate about the grey zone between black and white absolutes when it comes to complex human beings, the choices we make, and the actions we take.

Are morals and values absolute? Maybe what is right and wrong has to do with how we feel about ourselves after the fact? What do you think?

Think about this

Have you wondered about what makes morals better or worse? Is it our intentions, actions, or results, or some combination? In other words, when it comes to values, what really matters: what people want to do, what we actually do, or what happens because of what we do?

Over the years some have argued that human beings basically follow one simple rule: we pursue pleasure and avoid pain. Thus, the greater good means more happiness and less suffering. Morality is whatever increases overall wellbeing: the most value to the most people.

In this way of thinking, some believe that intention is not worth very much, decisions and actions are only moral if they benefit the majority most of the time, and that the ends justify the means. The outcomes of our actions are what determines their morality.

Do you believe that intention matters, or that actions matter, or that only results matter? And for whom? Does it always have to be the majority? What do you think?

Have you heard?

"The truth is that it is the greatest happiness of the greatest number that is the measure of right and wrong." Jeremy Bentham ~English utilitarian philosopher, legal scholar, and social reformer

What do you think he meant?

Light your path

Light your path with **Courage**. How do *you* define courage? How do you show it? Blaze a trail this way...

I am willing to try new things and take a risk for something important to me. I am not afraid of making mistakes; I learn from them. I am open and honest about what I believe, how I feel, and what is right. I am my own person and avoid doing things for the approval of others. If I believe in something, I take an interest in it, pursue it, and follow-through, regardless of what others might think. I don't observe life from the sidelines; I get active and get involved in causes that I believe in. I know fear is natural, and I feel fear like everyone else, but I don't let it get in the way of being who I am and following my dreams.

Pathways to **courage** come from a power within you. For example, if you would rather play music than baseball or softball, you practice the cello when others think you should practice your fielding and batting. Or if you believe in changing something for the better, such as your school's recycling program, you pursue it, even when it is not popular to do so or when others might disapprove. Or if you believe something is not right, such as the treatment of immigrant families in your community, you write a letter to the newspaper, or start a blog, or go door-to-door for a petition that you present to the city council.

Today try to do something bold that you have wanted to do for a while but have not yet tried.

Have you heard?

"Whatever you think you can do, or believe you can do, begin it, because action has magic, grace, and power in it." Johann Goethe ~German poet, dramatist, and philosopher

"I am not afraid of storms, for I am learning how to sail my ship." Louisa May Alcott ~American novelist and poet

What do you think they meant? Why do you think courage is so important? Why do courage and learning go hand-in-hand?

Did you know?

Courage is useful in competition.

Courage is even more useful in cooperation.

You can do bold things as an individual and with a team.

And did you know?

Helping others succeed helps you be great.

When you are a good teammate you will always win.

When you honor yourself and others, everyone can succeed.

What do these principles mean? How might they help you in walking your path?

Have you heard?

"Alone we can do so little; together we can do so much." Helen Keller
~American blind and deaf writer and teacher

What do you think she meant?

Haiku for you

In cold early spring

The earth and the birch whisper

As one we endure

Do you understand?

There was once a proud knight who was bothered by a question. He traveled for many days to find a great mage who lived in a secluded tower and who was considered the wisest person in the land.

The knight climbed the stairs to the top floor of the tower to find the mage meditating in his sanctuary. The knight shouted, "I have come to ask about heaven and hell. How do we know they exist?"

The mage glared at the knight and responded, "How dare you interrupt me. You are a sorry excuse for a warrior. You are rude, sloppy, and weak. Your armor and shield are wasted on you!"

In a fit of rage, the knight drew his sword to smite the mage with a mighty blow. Then the mage calmly smiled, causing the knight to stop just before striking him. The mage said, "Now you know hell."

The knight was shocked at his own behavior and fell to his knees, wept, and quietly said, "What have I done? My mission is to protect this land, help the poor, and be kind and compassionate to all."

The knight continued, "How could I have thought to harm you, though your words were ruthless and untrue. I will recommit my life to peace and justice." The mage then said, "Now you know heaven."

What does this story mean to you? What does it suggest about heaven and hell? What does it suggest about courage and humility?

Shine the light

There have been many great leaders who embodied the virtues of courage, compassion, and peace. One was Martin Luther King, Jr. an African-American civil rights activist and leader who said:

"Courage is the power of the mind to overcome fear. Our lives begin to end the day we become silent about the things that matter. The time is always right to do the right thing. Life's most persistent and urgent question is: what are you doing for others?"

What do you think he meant?

Check your reality

Sit very quietly and still. Take a few deep breaths. Do not move. Are you motionless right now? How do you know? As you sit still, think about the reality of the cosmos:

Right now, the earth is rotating on its axis. It is also slowly shifting on its axis. And it is orbiting very fast around the sun.

Right now, the sun, the earth, and our whole solar system is orbiting very fast around the center of our galaxy, the Milky Way.

Right now, the Milky Way is hurtling through space at an incredible speed because the universe is expanding.

You are not motionless at all! If you left a trail of smoke, it would look like a spinning top within an elliptical turning wheel within a corkscrew accelerating through space!

Do you understand? What is the difference between perception and experience?

True nature is

Hold a flower in your hand. For three minutes breathe deeply but easily. Look at the flower. Keep your attention on the flower. Enjoy the wonder that is a flower. Notice how thoughts drift in and out of your mind as you focus on the flower. Let them come and then drift away. Become aware *of your being aware* of the flower. **The flower just is.**

Stand in front of a tree. For three minutes breathe deeply but easily. Look at the tree. Keep your attention on the tree. Enjoy the wonder that is a tree. Notice how thoughts drift in and out of your mind as you focus on the tree. Let them come and then drift away. Become aware *of your being aware* of the tree. **The tree just is.**

What do you think is meant by true nature?

Light your path

Light your path with **Humility**. How do *you* define humility? How do you show it? Blaze a trail this way…

I let my actions speak for themselves. I achieve great things to achieve them, not for the acclaim. I have a realistic sense of my own talents and abilities. I notice and honor others for their ideas and achievements. I am different from others but not separate from them, and understand we are all equal as human beings. Having less or more material possessions than others does not define who I am. I avoid forcing my ideas on others or passing judgment on theirs. I listen more than I talk and don't need to be the center of attention. I am quietly proud of what I accomplish and what I have to offer. I have an open-mind to be teachable; I am always open to learning something new.

Pathways to **humility** come from a power within you. For example, if you are the fastest swimmer or most accomplished martial artist or best dancer, you take pride in your ability. But rather than talking about yourself, or your accomplishments, you notice and talk about how capable other people are, and honor their ideas, abilities, and possessions. You share your ideas, too, in the spirit of being open and inclusive, but know you do not need to talk about yourself to stand out. You let your ideas and achievements speak for themselves.

Today try to not talk about yourself: avoid using *I*, *me*, or *my* when you are speaking with others.

Have you heard?

"True modesty is the source of all virtue." Muhammad ~Arabian prophet and founder of Islam

"Humility isn't thinking less of yourself; it's thinking of yourself less." C. S. Lewis ~British poet, novelist, and theologian

What do you think they meant? Why are humility and modesty so important?

Change your mind

Use a new mindset to stay humble when tough surprises come along.

Stop using this frame: Why is this happening to me? I don't deserve it.

Start using this frame: What is happening? I am open to learn from it.

Did you know?

You are not any better or any worse than anyone else.

You are incredible and normal at the same time.

Each one of us is a center of the universe.

Think about what these principles mean. How might they help you walk your path?

Have you heard?

"Pride makes us artificial; humility makes us real." Thomas Merton ~American Trappist monk, spiritual mystic, and writer

"Remember that you are absolutely unique — just like everyone else." Margaret Mead ~American anthropologist and researcher

"Just be ordinary and nothing special." Shunryu Suzuki ~Japanese Zen master, teacher, and writer

What do you think they meant? What does it mean to be special but not different?

Around the world

Namaste

(pronounced *nah-mas-tay*)

Namaste is a Hindu term that originated from India and Nepal. It is a respectful form of greeting that is often spoken with a bow and hands pressed together, palms touching, and fingers pointed upward. It is commonly used with a relative, guest, or stranger.

Namaste means "the light of the spirit in me recognizes and honors the light of the spirit in you." A warm and welcoming gesture, it shows respect, courtesy, and peace, and is used in goodbyes as well. Namaste is also often used to express gratitude.

Think about this

Selfing is how we try to keep up with what others do or have. Resist competing for attention by trying to be the same but better. We don't need the *likes, friends, followers* and other currencies on social media. False self is how we "show up" when we care too much about what others think, want to be like them and popular, and want to stand out.

Selfing is promoting the way we look, or what we have, or what we've done. When others share too much on-line to get attention, why not remain a bit of a mystery and maintain good boundaries in our private lives? When we choose avatars to virtually represent ourselves, we can use healthy images that embody the characteristics of our true selves.

Rather than use social media to impress people, we can use it to impact them instead. Rather than post selfies, click on trendy tags, or troll unworthy memes, we can share creative ideas or ask thoughtful questions. **We can express our self-worth in meaningful ways**, not care about the approval of others, and show up as who we really are.

How much self-promotion do you do? What are some better ways to express yourself? What is meant by "showing up" as false self versus true self?

Have you heard?

"You must unlearn the habit of being someone else, of imitating the voices of others, and mistaking the faces of others as your own." Hermann Hesse ~German poet, novelist, philosopher, and painter

"Live life from the inside out rather than from the outside in." Parker Palmer ~American Quaker theologian and wisdom teacher and writer

What do you think he meant?

Check your reality

Have you noticed that in our age of information everywhere all the time we find it harder and harder to agree on the facts?

Social media and on-line sources give us an almost infinite number of ways to access and share information. These sources can share useful knowledge, but they can also be forces for misinformation and untruth.

And artificial intelligence increasingly makes it harder to distinguish fact from fiction through things like manipulated videos and augmented reality that can have fake or misleading content.

Technology can create the illusion that we are well-connected, well-informed, and have the facts. We must be vigilant, discerning, and careful about how and where we get good information and real news.

Do you understand? How do you make sure you are using good information?

Shine the light

As new messaging apps, chatrooms, and on-line forums come and go, sharing information between people keeps getting easier and faster.

Do new technologies always help us communicate better? Is it okay for them to replace face-to-face interactions? So many things seem to get lost in translation when we depend on impersonal or remote channels to talk to each other. The researcher, speaker, and author Brené Brown has said, "Technology has become a kind of imposter for connection, making us think we are connected when we're really not."

How meaningful are your connections and conversations with other people?

Did you know?

Communication is the foundation of friendship.

Honesty is the foundation of good communication.

And did you know?

We are most happy when we are with true friends.

The quality of life is dependent on good friendships.

Think about this

Friendship is vital to your wellbeing: friendship with yourself and with others. Good friends are encouraging, caring, and kind. They can safely share their thoughts and feelings and ask for help from one another. Good friends have fun together, laugh a lot, and can be themselves. They apologize when needed, make amends, and easily forgive.

Friendships are created from small moments that build trust over time. Think about what you expect from friends and what they expect from you. Your inner circle of friends should energize you. It is natural to feel lonely at times, so explore new friendships; widen your circles to meet new people. Invite your circles of friends to get together.

How might you be a better friend with yourself and with others? How might you develop higher quality friendships?

Have you heard?

"Friendships are discovered rather than made." Harriet Beecher Stowe ~American abolitionist and freedom activist:

What do you think she meant?

Shine the light

There have been great leaders who live the values of friendship, conversation, and equality. One is Margaret Wheatley, a leadership and business consultant, teacher, and author, who has written:

"I believe we can change the world if we start listening to one another again. Simple, truthful conversation where we each have a chance to speak, we each feel heard, and we each listen well. If we can talk about what is important to us, we come alive. Conversation takes time. We need time to sit together, to listen, to worry, and to dream together."

How might you start having higher quality conversations?

Do you understand?[1]

There was a girl who lived on a farm. One evening a violent storm came from across the plain. The next morning, she walked outside and was amazed at all the damage that had been done.

She thought about the night before, during the storm, when a friend had called and got angry with her for no reason. She was confused, but then remembered her friend had just broken up with her boyfriend.

She knew she was not the reason her friend was upset. She politely asked her friend to stop and said she would call her back the next day. She felt hurt, but let her feelings fade, knowing her friend was in pain.

Standing in the nearest field, the girl knew another storm would eventually come. She could not stop the next storm, and knew she was not responsible for the storms in other people's lives either.

When have you dealt with storms that are not about you? What did you do?

Did you know?

What people think about you is not your responsibility.

What people do is not because of you.

And did you know?

Do not rely on others to validate who you are.

No one can make you feel less-than without your permission.

Think about what these principles mean. What is meant by *without your permission*?

Have you heard?

"Don't take things personally; nothing people do or say is because of you." Don Miguel Ruiz ~Mexican spiritual Toltec teacher and writer

"Care about people's approval and you will become their prisoner." Lao-Tzu ~Chinese philosopher and father of Taoism

What do you think they meant? How do you "personalize" what other people do or say?

Do you understand?[2]

There was once a man who felt he was not worthy and so he went to a wise rabbi for advice. The man said, "I know I'm a fool, sir, but what should I do about it?"

The rabbi was very excited about the man's question and he exclaimed, "My son, if you know you are a fool, and admit to being a fool, then you are surely no fool."

The man responded, very confused, "I don't understand. If I'm not a fool, then why does everyone tell me I am? Why does everyone make fun of me and put me down?"

The rabbi pondered the man's question, and with a hint of mischief in his eyes, said, "If you believe you are a fool because of what other people say, well then you are a fool."

What does this story mean to you? What is the rabbi trying to say to the man?

Change your mind

Use a new mindset to help you avoid taking things personally.

Stop feeling responsible for what other people think, say, and do.

Start being responsible for what you think, say, and do.

Epigram I am

Strange as it may seem, when you make me feel bad,

I feel even worse that I'm the only one I can blame!

Check your reality

Have you noticed that we often see things differently and that what is real to one person may not be real to another?

A boy shows a girl a small, round, red fruit, and he asks, "What is it?"

She says, "It is an apple."

He laughs and says, "It is not an apple; it is a small, round, red fruit."

So she says, "Then it is a tomato."

He laughs again and says, "No, it is a small, round, red fruit."

She says, "Then it must be a pomegranate."

And he says, "I told you, it is just a small, round, red fruit."

Then they both laugh.

Another girl walks up. They show her the fruit and ask, "What is it?"

She looks at the fruit for a moment, and then *she takes a bite.*

Do you understand? What is the difference between perception and experience?

Have you heard?

"I sometimes confuse my thoughts about the world with the world itself." Paul Auster ~American novelist, poet, and essayist

What do you think he meant? Can you think of a time when this happened to you?

Did you know?

Our differences do not divide us.

How we perceive differences divides us.

Judgments about those differences is what divides us.

Think about what these principles mean. How might they help you walk your path?

Light your path

Light your path with **Equality**. How do *you* define equality? How do you show it? Blaze a trail this way…

I embrace the incredible diversity of life and the equality of all people. I accept people as they are. I appreciate the differences in people. They may look different, act in different ways, and believe in different things, but this doesn't make them more or less of a person. I treat differences as a way to connect *with* people rather than separate *from* them. I know they are having their own life experience, with all of its ups and downs, just like me. Judging others has more to do with my own state of mind than with them. I value my own beliefs but show interest and respect for those of others. Intolerance is a dark force in the world, and I oppose all forms of prejudice, discrimination, and hate.

Pathways to **equality** come from a power within you. For example, if one of your friends cannot go to a movie because of a religious holiday, you accept it, wish him a great day, and show an interest in the holiday he is celebrating. If a new girl at school wears very different clothes because of her cultural traditions, you try to get to know her regardless of what she is wearing. If one of your friends makes a racist comment, you respectfully disagree, attempt to learn more about why he said it, and discuss with him why all forms of bigotry are wrong.

Today, try to openly appreciate different viewpoints and beliefs from others and not judge or ignore them.

Have you heard?

"Let us empower ourselves with knowledge and shield ourselves with unity." Malala Yousafzai ~Pakistani humanitarian activist and survivor of terrorism

"Tolerance and compassion are qualities of fearless people." Paulo Coelho ~Brazilian lyricist, novelist, and spiritual teacher

"Love is the absence of judgment." The Dalai Lama ~Tibetan and Buddhist spiritual leader

What do you think they meant?

Shine the light

Wise young people embrace diversity and commit to equality. In her essay, *Underneath We're All the Same*, Amy Maddox of Indiana wrote:

"He prayed—it wasn't my religion. He ate—it wasn't what I ate. He spoke—it wasn't my language. He dressed—it wasn't what I wore. He took my hand—it wasn't the color of mine. But when he laughed—it was how I laughed, and when he cried—it was how I cried."

What do you think she meant?

Did you know?

Cruelty is weakness.

Love and kindness are strength.

The most courageous pursue equality for all.

Have you heard?

"Darkness cannot drive out darkness; only light can do that. Hate cannot drive out hate; only love can do that." Martin Luther King, Jr. ~African-American civil rights activist and leader

"No one is born hating another person because of the color of his skin, or his background, or his religion." Nelson Mandela ~South African civil rights leader and revolutionary

What did they mean? Why are tolerance and compassion related and so important?

Around the world

Maitri

(pronounced *my-tree*)

Maitri is an ancient Sanskrit term for making friends with oneself and others. It means friendliness. It is not about becoming a better person. Rather, it reflects a gentle and loving kindness for oneself and others.

Maitri means accepting one's own imperfections, not judging oneself, and not being preoccupied with promoting a certain self-image. This way, one joyfully experiences life with humility and an open heart.

Light your path

Light your path with **Loving-kindness**. How do *you* define it? How do you show it? Blaze a trail this way...

I love myself, my family, and my friends. I do nice things for them and care about their wellbeing. I understand that no family is perfect, and no friendship is perfect either. There will always be ups and downs, but I still show love and kindness to the ones I care about, especially when things are down. I make a point to be nice and kind to strangers, regardless of my mood. No matter what is going on inside me, I can still be kind to other people. I know that sometimes just being there for someone when they need it, and giving them my undivided attention, is an expression of love, and the most important thing I can do.

Pathways to **loving-kindness** come from a power within you. For example, if your brother breaks your new tablet, you forgive him and tell him how much you love him. If it was not an accident, you might be very angry, and that's perfectly okay, but you do not take what happened personally. His actions have nothing to do with you. You can be angry and love him unconditionally at the same time. Family members and also friends sometimes hurt each other; it is human nature. You can practice loving-kindness with people you care about even when you are angry and feel it is undeserved.

Today try to do several random acts of kindness for both friends and strangers without expecting anything in return.

Have you heard?

"Even after all this time, the sun never says to the earth *You owe me*. Look what happens with a love like that; it lights the whole sky." Hafiz ~Persian poet and theosopher

"The beginning of love is to let those we love be perfectly themselves, and not to twist them to fit our own image." Thomas Merton ~American Trappist monk, spiritual mystic, and writer

What did they mean? Why is it so important for loving-kindness to be given freely?

Shine the light

When we are loving and kind, our mind, body, and spirit are in harmony with our heart. This is the way of a heart-centered life.

We are able to love others only as much as we love ourselves. When we show kindness, tenderness, and friendliness to ourselves, we can show them to others too. This affection comes from a deep place in our heart.

Perhaps the most important thing we must do on our path is to respect, love, and trust ourselves. Believe this to be true with every breath you take. You are worthy. Feel it deep inside your chest and stomach.

It has been said that everything is magical when you see it with your heart. If your heart aches you are alive. If your heart pounds, you are alive. Open your heart to feel your feelings and fully experience life.

Sometimes what we know in our heart gets clouded over by doubts and fears that come from other people's opinions and judgments. These can be painful. But we can trust our heart's wisdom.

Open your heart and mind to what is in front of you right now. Listen to your heart. Trust what your heart is telling you. When your heart feels in tune with a decision, then you will know it is the right one.

Oscar Wilde, the Irish poet and playwright, once wrote, "The heart is made to be broken but not turned to stone." We can live our life whole-heartedly knowing we are worthy and resilient and human.

Sadness, loss, and pain are a natural part of life. Here is an ancient Sufi proverb that is helpful to remember: **When the heart weeps for what it has lost, the spirit laughs at what it has gained.**

How might you start listening more to your heart? How might you follow your heart? How might feelings of sadness in your heart help you grow spiritually?

Have you heard?

"You should listen to your heart and not the voices in your head." Matt Groening ~American cartoonist, animator, writer, and actor

"The only lasting beauty is the beauty of the heart." Rumi ~Persian poet and Sufi mystic

What do you think they meant?

Pathways

Part 2

Topics

Nutrition ~ Sensing ~ Learning

Awareness ~ Attention ~ Time ~ Presence

Think about this

Have you given much thought about the food you eat? Have you noticed the link between what you eat and how you feel?

Pay attention to what you eat. Eat less processed foods, fried foods, chips, candy, energy drinks, and sugary sodas and juices. Drink water and eat natural fruits, vegetables, nuts, fish, wholegrains, milk, and eggs. **Eat less food from a package or a box and more from the earth.**

Nutrition is one of the most important things in life. Poor nutrition can negatively affect how you feel, think, and act. A poor diet can contribute to mood swings and feeling hyper, aggressive, depressed, or anxious. **Eat to fuel your body, not to feed your emotions!**

It may sound strange, but your body is the only home where you will always live. You may live in circumstances where it's hard to eat healthy. Don't worry too much about this, just do your best to eat well. **Trying to eat well is a form of dignity and self-respect.**

A well-nourished body is very important for the wellbeing of your mind. There is a proven relationship. Good nutrition is linked to better sleep too. Good food is critical to developing healthy mind-body-spirit. **Eat healthy, exercise daily, and get enough sleep to be awesome!**

Have you heard?

"Let food be thy medicine." Hippocrates ~Greek pioneering physician and teacher, and the father of medicine

"No disease that can be treated by diet should be treated by any other means." Maimonides ~Spanish Jewish philosopher, Tora scholar, astronomer, and physician

What do you think they meant?

Check your reality

Have you noticed that we often see things differently and that what is real to one person may not be real to another?

Five brothers stand on a dock looking out at a beautiful blue lake.

Their father asks them, "What do you see?"

One brother says, "I see a lake that is very deep and good for fishing!"

Another brother says, "I see a lake with big waves for wakeboarding!"

The third brother says, "I see a lake with clear water for swimming!"

The next brother says, "I see a lake with wind that is good for sailing!"

The last brother does not say anything, and instead, *he jumps in.*

Do you understand? What is the difference between perception and experience?

Have you heard?

"What we have to learn to do we learn by doing." Aristotle ~Greek philosopher, scientist, and teacher

What do you think he meant?

Do you understand?

Twenty-five hundred years ago there lived two wise men. Socrates lived in the west in ancient Greece. Confucius lived in the east in ancient China. Both wise men had a profound impact on their world and on the future of philosophy, logic, and ethics. Both men challenged the people of their time to question the nature of government, morality, and justice. And both men were vilified by powerful politicians and wealthy individuals who did not want the status quo disrupted.

Early in his life Socrates distinguished himself as a warrior. Socrates loved to debate and ask people questions, and he challenged them to think for themselves and to pursue uncompromising truth. The great oracle of Delphi claimed Socrates was the wisest man in the world. He humbly responded he was wise only because he knew that he knew nothing at all. Others did not agree; his student Plato captured many of his teachings. His credo: **The unexamined life is not worth living**.

Early in his life Confucius distinguished himself as a statesman. Confucius loved to share stories with people to get them thinking for themselves about morals, proper behavior, and good manners. He was also humble and believed that cultivating virtue begins with curiosity. Like Socrates, he never wrote anything down, but others captured his questioning nature and the thoughtfulness of his teachings. His credo: **What you do not wish for yourself, do not do unto others.**

What did these men have common? Why do you think they were considered so wise?

Have you heard?

"True wisdom comes to each of us when we realize how little we understand about life, ourselves, and the world around us." Socrates ~Greek philosopher, ethicist, and teacher

"To know what you know and what you do not know, that is true knowledge." Confucius ~Chinese wisdom teacher and philosopher

What do you think they meant?

Shine the light

We learn in many different ways. We are always learning. We can pay attention to the quality of our sources of learning.

We learn from using our senses: what we see, hear, smell, taste, and feel. We learn through tradition: the rituals and customs in our family and community.

We learn from example: the behaviors and actions of others. We learn from our own experiences: participation in a variety of activities. We learn from instruction: the study of information and knowledge from expert sources.

And very importantly, we learn from studying history: we cannot fully understand our current world or effectively shape the future without understanding our past.

It has been suggested by teachers over the years that wisdom comes from observation, experience, study, and introspection.

How do you like to learn? How do you seek out ways to learn that help you the most?

Check your reality

Have you thought about how much of the world you actually see?

Light waves travel in many different wavelengths. We see less than one-percent of the electromagnetic spectrum. It seems we can only see a tiny portion of reality with our naked eye.

And we can see the same thing in totally different ways. We can use a microscope to zoom-in or use a telescope to zoom-out. It seems reality presents itself differently depending on the magnification.

What does this mean for how you perceive reality? What about sound, touch, and smell?

Epigram I am

As long as I want to see something a certain way

I can't see it for what it is!

Think about this

There is constant demand for and fragmenting of our attention.

We are conditioned to respond to many kinds of constant interruption, and this makes it very hard to concentrate. Different forms of media and social media are designed to grab our attention and distract us from focusing on what is important.

How often do you find yourself skimming an article instead of actually reading it? How often do you find yourself text messaging instead of having a real conversation? How often do you find yourself trying to do several things at once but feeling like none get done very well?

We can pay attention to our attention: a relaxed attention or a focused concentration. Either way, we can stop checking messages all the time, start having full interactions with people, turn off our mobile devices, and make time for deep reading and thinking.

How might you pay more attention to one thing at a time and not get so distracted?

Have you heard?

"I think we are blind. Blind people who can see, but do not see." Jose Saramago ~Portuguese novelist and philosopher

What do you think he meant? Why do you think being awake and alert is so important?

Do you understand?[3]

In a desert village several disciples were sitting in a circle talking with their master, one of the town's elder mullahs. One of the disciples asked, "Can you give me a word of wisdom to guide me through the day?" It was the mullah's day of silence, so he wrote on a pad of paper, "Awareness" and gave it to the student, who looked a little confused.

Another disciple said, "Master, that's too brief. Can you expand on that a bit?" The mullah then wrote on the pad, "Awareness, Awareness." The disciples were now getting a little uneasy. So a third student said, "Master, what does that mean?" The mullah wrote on the pad one more time, "Awareness, Awareness, Awareness — means Awareness!"

What does this story mean to you? What was the mullah trying to teach his students?

Light your path

Light your path with **Awareness**. How do *you* define awareness? How do you show it? Blaze a trail this way...

I am aware of the world around me in its infinite wonder and beauty. I am alert and don't get distracted easily. I do not obsess about what happened yesterday or what might happen tomorrow. I give people my full attention when I am with them. I am present and actively listen and connect with them in a sincere manner. I observe how I interact with people and the world in general, and this helps me pay attention to what I'm thinking, feeling, and doing in this moment right now. I study what is going on within me and around me to fully experience life. The lamp of awareness helps me see the path unfolding before me.

Pathways to **awareness** come from a power within you. For example, you pay less attention to your smartphone and more attention to where you are and who you're with. When you are in class or at lunch with friends or walking somewhere, you put your device away. Unplug it throughout the day and have real conversations with people. When you play a video game or a game app on your mobile, stop the game sometimes, sit quietly, take a few deep breaths, look around, and enjoy the stillness of the moment. Experience life without it glued to a screen.

Today try to observe as many of the small details of your surroundings as you can wherever you are.

Have you heard?

"Awareness is like the sun. When it shines on things, they are transformed" Thich Nhat Hanh ~Vietnamese Buddhist monk and spiritual leader

"Learning is the only thing the mind never exhausts, never fears, and never regrets." Leonardo da Vinci ~Italian artist, writer, and inventor

What do you think they meant? Why are being awake and alert so important?

Haiku for you

On the mountain trail

I can see the whole, still world

Alert in my joy

Check your reality

Have you noticed we often don't pay full attention to what is going on around us?

A student asked the teacher how to be more present.

The teacher said, "Stop."

Another student asked the teacher how to be more present.

The teacher said, "Look."

Another student asked the teacher how to be more present.

The teacher said, "Listen."

One last student asked the teacher how to be more present.

The teacher then smiled.

And took a deep breath.

Do you understand? What does it feel like to be fully aware of the present moment?

True nature is

Listen to your favorite song. During the song, breathe deeply but easily. Focus only on the song. See the music in your mind; envision the rhythm as beautiful, colorful waves flowing in space.

Look at a favorite photograph. Breathe deeply and understand the amazing connection you have with the world. Think about why this snapshot makes you feel a certain way.

What do you think is meant by true nature?

Change your mind

Use a new mindset to better handle all the waiting you do every day.

Stop being angry, agitated, or frustrated because you are wasting time.

Start observing, reflecting on, and appreciating everything around you.

Did you know?

There is something we all have called beginner's mind.

It means seeing the world with open wonder.

We are free to see the world as it really is right now.

And did you know?

Yesterday and tomorrow are not real.

Today is the only reality.

Awareness is being right here right now.

Think about what these principles mean. How might they help you walk your path?

Have you heard?

"Forever is composed only of nows." Emily Dickinson ~American poet

"Be here now." Ram Dass ~American spiritual wisdom teacher and writer

What do you think they meant?

Around the world

Hygge

(pronounced *hoo-gah*)

Hygge originates from the Scandinavian country of Denmark. It means a feeling or situation that is cozy, comforting, bringing contentment. It often occurs when a seemingly ordinary moment feels very special.

Hygge involves doing simple, calming activities that require little effort, like reading a book by candlelight or playing a board game with friends by a warm fire. It is enjoying these moments at your leisure.

Think about this

Wise people from around the world have questioned the nature of time for centuries. Time is a very tricky concept. Scientists and philosophers have spent a lot of time thinking about time!

An old clever saying sums up how many of us perceive time: **Today is the tomorrow we were worrying about yesterday**.

Understand that right now is the only real time. By being present—some have called it *being in the now*—we can avoid the stress and strain of dwelling in the past or worrying about the future.

Do not look back and be troubled about the past, because it is gone forever. This doesn't mean that we should forget the past. In fact, we can and should learn from the past, but it does not help to dwell there.

Do not be too concerned about the future, because it has not yet happened. This doesn't mean that we should not look to the future and set goals or imagine good things and new experiences that could be.

When we are young, we have a strange sense of time. A few days can feel like an eternity and yet we make the excuse of never having enough time! **Time is never about time; it's always about priority.**

In Latin, *carpe diem* means *seize this day*. We can seize it by setting a few simple priorities for the day and doing our best.

How we live today determines the quality of tomorrow. Rather than worry about time, we can make time—that is, make it a priority—to be thoughtful about life and experience and enjoy it one day at a time.

Why do you think it is so important to be present, to be in the now? What happens when you are not present, when you spend too much time in the past or future?

Have you heard?

"Time is an illusion. This moment right now is the only real time." Eckhart Tolle ~German-Canadian spiritual wisdom writer and teacher

"Take care of each moment and you take care of all time." Siddhartha Gautama ~the Buddha, Indian mystic and founder of Buddhism

"Eternal life belongs to those who live in the present." Ludwig Wittgenstein ~Austrian-British philosopher of logic and language

What did they mean? What is it about time that is so interesting?

Do you understand?[4]

A young woman was struggling with many perceived difficulties in her life, so she went to a wise counselor for help. She asked, "How can I handle all these problems? Why is my life such a mess?"

The counselor responded, "We can handle the challenges of today. It is when we feel the burden of two eternities, yesterday and tomorrow, that we can break down. It is not the problems of today that drive us mad. It is the distraction from what happened yesterday, or the dread of what might happen tomorrow. Are you living in the moment?"

She nodded, "No." The counselor went on, "This day is fresh with possibility. We can let go of the past and look forward to the future, but the book of life is blank today. Write your story one page at a time."

What was he trying to say?

Have you heard?

"Give every day the chance to become the most beautiful of your life. There is nothing that cannot happen today." Mark Twain ~American journalist, novelist, and humorist

What do you think he meant? Do you make the most of each day? Do you see the beauty and greatness in each day?

Check your reality

Have you noticed that we are often bothered by things in the past or future and do not enjoy what we are doing right now?

A girl and her friend are eating dinner at her friend's house. The girl says she is unhappy that her teacher at school does not treat her fairly.

Her friend says, "Is that so?"

Then the girl says she is very excited about a new movie coming out, but she's not sure if a boy that she likes will ask her to go.

Her friend says, "Is that so?"

Then the girl says she is very upset that her dad only allows her to watch one hour of television a night.

Her friend says, "Is that so?"

Then the girl says she is very upset that her mom won't buy her a pair of very trendy, but expensive, shoes that she wants.

Her friend says, "Is that so?"

The girl wonders how she will ever be happy with so many worries. Her friend then says, "Enjoy your meal and then wash your plate."

What is the girl so concerned about and why? What is her friend trying to tell her?

Change your mind

Use a new mindset to better stay mindful in the present moment.

Stop future-tripping: don't make-up stories about the future.

Start day-dwelling: stay focused on a simple agenda for this day.

Did you know?

If you feel depressed, you are living in the past.

If you feel anxious, you are living in the future.

If you feel peaceful, you are living in the now.

And did you know?

The past is history.

The future is a mystery.

Today is a gift called the present.

Think about what these principles mean. Do they suggest that you should not learn from the past or set goals for the future?

Shine the light

Sanskrit is an ancient tradition and language in Hinduism and Buddhism. Consider reflecting on this ancient Sanskrit prayer:

Look to this day
For it is life,
The very life of life.
Yesterday is but a dream
And tomorrow is only a vision,
But today, well-lived,
Makes every yesterday a dream of happiness
And every tomorrow a vision of hope.
Look well, therefore,
To this day.

What does this prayer mean to you?

Haiku for you

Yesterday is gone

Like the wind from the high desert

Today, ocean breeze

Think about this

Have you noticed how time can disappear? When we immerse ourselves in an activity that is both challenging and worthwhile, time seems to stand still. Maybe it speeds up. Either way, we lose track of it!

When we lose track of time, we are often doing something we love to do, like compete in a sport, play music, or read a good book. Our awareness of time goes away for a while. We are in the flow of life.

We lose our sense of time, and we can lose sense of our surroundings. **We are concentrating on one thing.** It usually means we are doing something we enjoy and stretching our abilities. We are in-the-zone.

We should be careful, however, about *zoning-out*. Time feels like it flies when we watch television shows or play video games because we are in a trance of sorts. We are hypnotized, lost in a daze of little value.

Instead, we can choose *zoning-in* on productive activities. It is much more fulfilling to focus on a project that has inherent value, like building a treehouse, and that gives a lasting sense of accomplishment.

In a letter to his son, Albert Einstein wrote, "Play the things on the piano that please you—that is the way to learn best, doing something with such enjoyment you don't even notice that time passes."

We don't always need to have the goal of losing time, but we can pay attention to when it happens. If we invest more time and energy in zoning-in rather than zoning-out, we will be more happy and fulfilled.

When have you experienced losing your sense of time or surroundings in the flow of life?

Epigram I am

Knowing that the only real time is now, I spend each moment

worrying about what is going to happen to it!

Shine the light

William Blake was an English poet. Consider a verse of this poem, *Auguries of Innocence,* **he once wrote:**

To see a world in a grain of sand
And a heaven in a wildflower
Hold infinity in the palm of your hand
And eternity in an hour

Rainer Maria Rilke was a German poet and novelist. Consider a verse of this poem, *Buddha in Glory,* **he once wrote:**

A billion stars going spinning through the night
Glittering above your head
But in you is the presence that will be
When all the stars are dead

What do these poems mean to you? What similar ideas are they both trying to describe?

Pathways

Part 3

Topics

Positive attitude ~ Patience ~ Pause and effect

Creativity and self-expression ~ Determination ~ Resilience

Acceptance ~ Self-awareness ~ Power

Letting go ~ Gratitude ~ Simplicity ~ Discernment

Dignity ~ Self-worth ~ Responsibility

Light your path

Light your path with a **Positive attitude**. How do *you* define positive attitude? How do you show it? Blaze a trail this way...

I see the goodness in each moment of the day. I see the goodness in myself. Even when things seem bad, I can see the good. I treat problems and challenges as opportunities. I find joy in the small things of life. I am open to the wonders of this world and am ready to meet the challenges before me. I am optimistic when others around me are not and do not let other people or events get me down. I choose my own attitude and understand that life is a state of mind. While I usually can't control what happens, I can control how I respond. I am able to easily adapt. I remind myself of the incredible gift it is to be alive.

Pathways to **positive attitude** come from a power within you. For example, if your soccer game is cancelled because of a rainstorm, you are not upset because you know the rainwater brings needed life. If you do not get a good grade on an exam, you know it is a learning experience to help you do better in the future. If a close friend forgets your birthday, you smile and remind yourself that there is no need to be bothered by the little things. Your love of life comes from inside.

Today try to avoid saying anything negative or critical to another person in any situation.

Have you heard?

"Pessimism leads to weakness; optimism to power." William James ~American pioneer in psychology, philosophy, and pragmatism

"A person can change his future merely by changing his attitude." Oprah Winfrey ~American entertainer, actress, and business leader

What do you think they meant?

Do you understand?

There was a humble young man who lived in a modest house and was studying to become a music teacher. One day a neighbor angrily knocked on his door, told the man that his dog had been roaming free on the neighbor's property, and pushed the dog into the man's house. The man smiled, gladly accepted the dog, and cared for it with much love. He made sure the dog no longer roamed his neighbor's property.

A few months later, the neighbor knocked on his door again — this time more politely — and said he had been mistaken and was sorry. The dog was actually a stray whose owner had left the area but was now back. The man smiled, gladly returned the dog, and said he hoped the owner would better care for it and not allow it to roam on the neighbor's property. Then the young man happily returned to his music studies.

What does this story mean? Why is he so accepting of caring for a dog that was not his?

Did you know?

Being positive involves keeping things in perspective.

It is quite easy to get rid of the negative thoughts in your mind.

Dwelling on what can't happen isn't helpful since anything is possible.

Think about what these principles mean. How might they help you walk your path?

Have you heard?

"Do not dwell for a single moment on any kind of negative thought."
Emmet Fox ~American spiritual wisdom teacher, speaker, theologian

"If I cannot do great things, I can do small things in a great way."
Martin Luther King, Jr. ~African-American civil rights activist, leader

What do you think they meant? How easy is it to stop dwelling on negative thoughts?

Change your mind

Use a new mindset to create a solid foundation for daily living.

Stop trying to make quantum leaps with quick and easy big wins.

Start making small moves, taking small steps, to achieve lasting results.

Light your path

Light your path with **Patience**. How do *you* define patience? How do you show it? Blaze a trail this way…

I stay calm and relaxed when dealing with a difficult situation or challenging person. I take my time and don't create needless tension or anxiety. I understand that most activities don't have to be done so fast or with so much urgency. I am comfortable waiting and tolerate delays without getting frustrated. I allow events to unfold as they are meant to, and appreciate a nice, steady pace to life. I avoid trying to control situations and see the value of going with the flow. I know the most meaningful things in life usually take a while.

Pathways to **patience** come from a power within you. For example, whether dealing with your parents' rules, getting your driver's license, or wanting the school year to end, be at ease with waiting. Life is long. You will likely live to be over ninety years old! Why rush into things? In a society built for speed, we still perceive things as too slow. Why hurry so much? Free yourself by changing perspective. Pay attention to each moment and value your experience no matter what is going on.

Today try to breathe deeply, relax your body, take it easy, and smile whenever you feel impatient or anxious.

Have you heard?

"All things pass. Patience attains all that it strives for." Teresa of Avila ~Sainted Spanish mystic, Christian nun, and reformer

"Patience is the companion of wisdom." Augustine of Hippo ~Sainted African-Berber Christian theologian and philosopher

What do you think they meant?

Think about this

Whatever we are doing, we can do our best, and think through difficult situations before deciding what to do. If a negative thought arises, we can observe it, not judge it, let it go, and then return our attention to what needs to be done. We are not responsible for our first thought, but we are responsible for our second.

We will encounter many things that frustrate or irritate us. As we walk our path, we will experience detours, delays, and dead-ends. We will be tested by obstacles that might block us from doing what we want to do. We may even be seriously wronged or harmed.

It is not helpful to be impulsive: to run from problems or rush into solutions. There is a difference between *reactive* and *responsive*. Reactive is thoughtless; responsive is thoughtful. This is the important art of pause and effect. **We can put space between thought and action.**

If we are angry, we think about why we are angry. Will anger or hatred solve our problem? It's okay to be angry, but we can pause for a moment, feel the anger, even smile at it, and then let it go. Talking about it with someone helps. This clears our mind to find a solution.

If we feel helpless in a situation, we can ask for help. We don't need to struggle on our own. We can talk to a friend, a relative, a teacher, a counselor, or some other person we trust. We are not alone. We are not weak asking for help; rather, we are brave.

All things pass in time; time helps heal all wounds. With calm patience, deliberate effort, and a positive attitude, we really can overcome or achieve just about anything. An old Arab proverb reminds us we have the power: **The nature of rain is the same, but it makes thorns grow in the marsh and flowers in the garden.**

What is meant by the art of pause and effect? Why is it better to overcome adversity through positive action rather than negative anger?

Have you heard?

"The art of pausing in life is the most essential thing to learn." Anam Thubten ~Tibetan Buddhist, spiritual leader, writer, and teacher

How easy is it to do this? How might you practice this?

Light your path

Light your path with **Creativity**. How do *you* define creativity? How do you show it? Blaze a trail this way...

I use my imagination to make, build, invent, and create. I express myself with original music, art, ideas, stories, or other creations, without concern for whether I am good at it or what others might think. I avoid self-criticism and perfectionism. I show courage to try something new and create the way I want to. I let things flow, trust the natural process of creating, and enjoy the experience. I notice all the instructions and rules that say things should be done a certain way, and I resist conforming, enjoy improvising, and like trying new methods. I look for new and cool ways to do assignments at school, solve difficult problems, and complete projects. I notice the creative beauty that is everywhere in the world around me.

Pathways to **creativity** come from a power within you. For example, you love to immerse yourself in other worlds, maybe in a great book you are reading or in an adventure game you are playing. You can imagine other worlds, maybe with dragons, or vampires, or witches, or rock stars, or superheroes, or secret agents. It's not nerdy, it's creative! You can create your own new worlds through playing music, writing, crafting, painting, or other artistic activities.

Today try to create something new without worrying about it being cool, good, or original.

Have you heard?

"A joyful life is an individual creation that cannot be copied from a recipe." Mihaly Csikszentmihalyi ~Hungarian-American psychologist

"Creativity is intelligence having fun." Albert Einstein ~German-American physicist, teacher, and philosopher

What do you think they meant? Why do you think creativity is so important?

Did you know?

We are all born creative.

We need to express ourselves.

We need to create to feel fully alive.

And did you know?

Wandering and wondering are needed.

Imagining and daydreaming are desired.

Exploring and experimenting are required.

Think about what these principles mean. How might they help you walk your path?

Have you heard?

"You shall create beauty not to excite the senses but to nourish the soul." Gabriela Mistral ~Chilean poet, educator, feminist, and diplomat

"What great thing ever came into existence that was not first a fantasy." Carl Jung ~Swiss psychotherapist and pioneer in psychology

What do you think they meant?

Shine the light

Creativity is one of the most important qualities of being human. There are many ways to get creative. The key is to just get started.

There are many sources of creativity that can be inspirational for you such as interests, passions, hobbies, feelings, places, people, dreams, vacations, and other experiences.

Some of the infinite ways to be creative include storytelling, drawing, painting, music, drama, film, programming, poetry, cooking, photography, building, crafting, and decorating.

To get started, think about what you love to do, how you feel, where you've been, and what you've experienced. What comes to mind?

How are you creative? How might you make more of an effort to use your creativity?

Light your path

Light your path with **Determination**. How do *you* define it? How do you show it? Blaze a trail this way…

I take initiative to do what needs to be done. I believe in myself but also believe in asking for help. I stay connected to people I can learn from. I'm resourceful and utilize a variety tools and other resources to achieve my goals. When it's time to work on a challenging activity or project, I figure out how to get it done, work hard, and follow-through. I show grit and believe in preparation and practice to build my skills. When I believe in a cause, or a purpose, I pursue it with enthusiasm. I get excited about a seemingly impossible task or worthwhile cause and commit to completing the mission. I use my imagination, adapt to changing situations, and have fun not knowing how to do something

Pathways to **determination** come from a power within you. For example, if you want to be the lead role in the school play, you are willing to ask for help from the drama teacher in getting ready and find ways to study the techniques of other actors. If you believe you can be the captain of the hockey team, you are willing to do what it takes, like getting extra hours on the ice on weekends. If you wish to fight poverty in your community, you volunteer at the local food shelf and apply what you learn to help feed more people who are hungry. If you want to do really well on a college aptitude exam, you find the best preparation tools on-line and start a study group with friends.

Today try to ask for and accept help from another person and then show them gratitude.

Have you heard?

"Being willing is not enough, we must do." Leonardo da Vinci ~Italian artist, writer, and inventor

"Do or not do, there is no try." Yoda ~Jedi Grand Master from a galaxy far, far away

What do you think they meant? How are willingness and determination related?

Have you heard?

"Without a struggle there can be no progress." Frederick Douglass ~African-American leader, abolitionist, statesman

"It is under the greatest adversity that there exists the greatest potential for doing good, both for oneself and for others." The Dalai Lama ~Tibetan and Buddhist spiritual leader

"It is kind of fun to do the impossible." Walt Disney ~American entrepreneur, film producer, and pioneer in animation

What do you think they meant? What is the main theme they are trying to tell you?

Shine the light

Many different forms of creative art inspire us to overcome adversity.

Bob Marley was a Jamaican singer, songwriter, and musician, and spiritual Rastafarian, who sang these famous and uplifting lyrics:

"Get up, stand up, stand up for your rights! Get up, stand up, don't give up the fight! Get up, stand up, now you see the light!"

What do you think he meant? What did he mean about *the fight*?

Haiku for you

I walk deftly through

Shining fields of potential

Rich pastures of choice

Light your path

Light your path with **Resilience**. How do *you* define resilience? How do you show it? Blaze a trail this way...

I am strong and determined, and don't give up. I am adaptable to changing circumstances. I don't dwell on the problem; I find a solution. I finish what I start. I can rebound from things that cause pain and hardship, and don't let difficult experiences get me down. I work hard and take personal responsibility to do my best. I stand up for what I believe. I'm open to feedback on how I perform, don't take it personally, and avoid getting defensive. I learn from input to improve. I'm comfortable asking for help and ask for help when I need it.

Pathways to **resilience** come from a power within you. For example, if a family member is very sick—maybe a parent or a sibling who has cancer—you do what it takes to help out, even though it is hard. You don't let this get in the way of you taking good care of yourself. It may not feel fair that you have responsibilities your friends don't have. But you are determined to stay healthy, go to school or work, spend time with friends when possible, and do what you can to help your family.

Today try to complete a few small but important things you've been avoiding or procrastinating about.

Have you heard?

"There is no magic to achievement. It is really about hard work, choices, and persistence." Michelle Obama ~African-American First Lady and lawyer, writer, and speaker

"It is not the strongest who survive, nor the most intelligent, but those who are the most responsive to change." Charles Darwin ~English naturalist and pioneer of evolution science

"What stands in the way becomes the way." Marcus Aurelius ~Roman emperor, Stoic philosopher, and writer

What did they mean? Why are being flexible, adaptive, and resilient so important?

Think about this

You are great just the way you are. You may not believe this is true, but you are. This does not mean you are perfect. Nor does it mean you are better than or any more special than anyone else.

On the path, you will make mistakes and make poor decisions. You will find that you have limitations, just like everyone else. It does not matter if sometimes you say, or do, the "wrong" thing.

You may struggle at school or work when completing assignments or studying for tests. You may have difficulty concentrating as well as others. Whatever challenges you face, they do not define who you are.

The key is to be friendly with yourself. There is an old saying, an ancient Confucian proverb, that is a good reminder of the importance of being friendly with yourself: **Wherever you go, there you are.**

Do not judge yourself harshly, and do not blame yourself or others when difficulties arise. Avoid feeling sorry for yourself because it is not helpful. It's natural to feel down sometimes but avoid self-pity.

Joumana Haddad, a Lebanese poet, journalist, and women's rights activist, once wrote, "As for the errors I make, the only punishment I acknowledge for having made them is my awareness of them."

You are just right the way you are: perfectly human. Be kind and gentle with yourself. Be comfortable with who you are. **Self-awareness and self-acceptance are essential to your resilience and peace of mind**.

Do you agree that you can fully accept yourself while also wanting to improve?

Have you heard?

"In the midst of winter, I learned there was in me an invincible summer." Albert Camus ~French-Algerian philosopher, journalist, essayist, and novelist

"Failure is impossible." Susan B. Anthony ~American social reformer and women's rights activist

"Wherever you stumble, there your treasure lies." Joseph Campbell ~American mythologist and spiritual wisdom writer

What do you think they meant?

Shine the light

Perfectionism can get in the way of learning and growth. It can be a very unhealthy approach to school, work, friendships, or anything.

We can be too demanding of our ourselves and of others. We can be too critical as well. We can try too hard to be perfect based on someone else's expectations or who we think we should be to be accepted or successful. Perfectionism puts way too much pressure on ourselves.

We fail because we are human. It is natural to experience failure. But failure is not really failure; situations that seem like failure are simply opportunities to learn and grow. This is a cliché but absolutely true. Lessons in life probably come more from "failure" than "success."

True failure is not trying in the first place. If we need to be perfect, and are paralyzed by fear of failure, then we won't try at all. That is the real definition of failure. There is a saying: **A comfort zone is a wonderful place, but nothing ever grows there**.

Life is a process full of twists and turns. Things don't always work out the way we want. We do our best and things turn out differently than expected. Things don't go as planned. The best question is always the same: What did I learn? So the opposite of perfectionism is growth.

Growth is to say we made a mistake, or we were wrong, and to laugh at ourselves a bit; freedom to learn and grow and dare to try again.

How might you reframe failure and become more comfortable with it?

Have you heard?

"Failure is an important part of growth and developing resilience. Do not be afraid to fail." Michelle Obama ~African-American First Lady and lawyer, writer, and speaker

"Don't aim to be perfect! Aim to be antifragile. Never exhibit self-pity. Do not complain." Nassim Taleb ~Lebanese American risk analyst, statistician, and writer.

What did they mean? How can obstacles actually become the way forward?

Do you understand?

There was a young woman who went to a yoga instructor every week in the center of a busy and noisy city. Her instructor had endured terrible hardships in her life, not of her own making, but every time the girl arrived for a session, the instructor was calm and tranquil with a smile on her face. During the session, however, the instructor would become fierce and uncompromising, and push her to the limit.

One day she asked the instructor what the secret was to her serenity. Her instructor said, "I have learned how to have a conversation with myself. I was willing to create the time and space to talk to myself as a kind friend. These conversations help me become a spiritual warrior." The girl asked what that meant. The instructor then said, "My love and acceptance of life gives me the courage, strength, and hope I need."

What does this story mean to you?

Have you heard?

"It does not matter what happens; what matters is how we relate to our experience." Tara Brach ~American spiritual writer and teacher

"The place to improve the world is first in one's own heart, head, and hands." Robert Pirsig ~American novelist, philosopher, and teacher

"When we are no longer able to change a situation, we are challenged to change ourselves." Victor Frankl ~Austrian psychologist, Holocaust survivor, and writer

What did they mean? Why is it often better to change the way you react to things?

Think about this

Accept your situation right now and the world around you. Things may not be perfect, and they rarely are, but accept them for what they are right now. The world is changing, your path is unfolding, but reality may not be what you think is right or how you want it to be.

If you are uncomfortable, upset, or anxious, it is probably because you are having a hard time accepting a person, place, or situation, something in your life that is disturbing you. Open up and share your feelings with a close friend or family member about it. Then reflect on the situation to make an intentional decision about what to do.

If you recognize what is bothering you, first accept it as is. Then decide if you *want* to change it, and whether you *can* change it. You can also *change your reaction to it*. Sometimes it's better to change your thinking about the problem and adapt to the situation. **You always have two options: Accept it and change it or accept it and change you.**

Over a thousand years ago, Shantideva, the Indian Buddhist monk and scholar, summed up this approach perfectly when he said, "Why be unhappy about something if it can be remedied? And what is the use of being unhappy about something if it cannot be remedied?"

Why is acceptance the key to getting rid of most problems in your life? What does it mean to *change your reaction to it*?

Have you heard?

"We are disturbed not by what happens to us, but by our thoughts about what happens." Epictetus ~Greek slave and Stoic philosopher

"We cannot change anything until we accept it first." Carl Jung ~Swiss psychotherapist and pioneer in psychology

What do you think they meant? Does the second quote also include changing yourself?

Epigram I am

If I cannot accept my situation, then I need to figure out how

to accept my non-acceptance!

Did you know?

There is rarely just one right answer to a problem.

Every obstacle in life is really an opportunity in disguise.

Letting go can be more powerful than trying to be in control.

Think about what these principles mean. How might they help you walk your path?

Have you heard?

"Whenever I throw reality out the door it always comes back in through the window." Ashleigh Brilliant ~English-American humorist

"Life is what happens to you while you are making other plans." John Lennon ~English songwriter, singer, musician, and social activist

What do you think they meant?

Do you understand?

Once there were two very faithful monks. They had devoted their lives to living in a sanctuary where an important rule was that they could not interact with people outside of their holy place.

One day they were out walking on a road in a heavy rain and one of the monks, named Jampa, helped an elderly woman cross a muddy intersection. He carried her on his back so she would not get dirty.

The other monk, Choden, said nothing, but later down the road he told Jampa he was upset Jampa had carried the old woman on his back, given their oath to avoid contact with people in the village.

Jampa responded by asking Choden what he was talking about. Choden was confounded that Jampa did not even remember the woman and reminded him of the woman he helped cross the road.

Jampa, now remembering, looked at him and said that he had dropped her several miles back at the other end of the intersection. And then he asked Choden why he was still carrying her.

What does this story mean to you? Why is it important sometimes to "drop" what you are carrying? Why is it so hard to do sometimes?

Shine the light

Letting go does not mean that we become indifferent or apathetic to life. To let go actually means to take action:

Talk less and listen more.
Worry less and relax more.
Control less and accept more.
Criticize less and respect more.

What are some other *active* ways to let go?

Did you know?

It is not possible to be liked by everyone.

It is not realistic to always know why someone dislikes you.

It is not necessary to be liked by everyone to be whole.

And did you know?

If you are honest and humble, people will respect you.

You do not need their acceptance or approval.

Accept how someone feels about you knowing you are not to blame.

Think about what these principles mean. How might they help you walk your path?

Change your mind

Use a new mindset to handle difficult or challenging situations.

Stop trying to fix everything that is broken or solve every problem.

Start letting more situations unfold fluidly and resolve themselves.

Light your path

Light your path with **Gratitude**. How do *you* define gratitude? How do you show it? Blaze a trail this way...

I thank the world every day for who I am, what I have, and the world around me. I am very thankful for the gift of life. While I may not have everything I want or need, I am grateful each day for what I do have and for what I'm able to do. I do not feel entitled to having more or doing more. I truly appreciate the people in my life, the experiences I get, and the opportunities before me. I know the impact of a thank you.

Pathways to **gratitude** come from a power within you. For example, when your friend flies on an airplane to go on vacation while your family stays home, you hope your friend enjoys her trip. When she returns, you ask her about the trip. What did she learn, what did she experience? You understand that you can be as happy as she is with your own experiences. You can be grateful for your time at home and also for her trip abroad.

Today tell three people how and why you are grateful for them being in your life.

Have you heard?

"If the only prayer you ever say in your life is *thank you*, it will be enough." Meister Eckhart ~German monk, philosopher, and mystic

"Gratitude unlocks the fullness of life." Melody Beattie ~American spiritual writer and wellness teacher

What do you think they meant?

Shine the light

Tecumseh was a Native American Chief of the Shawnee nation. Reflect on one of the prayers he was known to say:

Live your life so that the fear of death can never enter your heart.
When you arise in the morning, give thanks for the morning light.
Give thanks for your strength, for your food, for the joy of living.
And if you see no reason for giving thanks, the fault is in yourself.

What does this prayer mean to you?

Think about this

Showing gratitude each day has many positive benefits. These include feeling more serene and happy, and less anxious or sad. It is helpful to remind ourselves how fortunate we are for the sacred life we have.

It is easy to fall into the trap of entitlement: the belief we don't have enough or are owed the things we want. It is human to want things to be different or want more. This is a negative mindset of "not enough."

If we show appreciation each day, we develop what some people call an **attitude of gratitude**. It is more like a habit, or a practice. Each day we can spend a few minutes thinking about what we are grateful for.

Each morning we might pick one or two ordinary things to be thankful for, such as our health, food, friends, parents, talent, or opportunity. We should avoid choosing any luxury, like a car or a video game.

We share our gratitude to make it come alive: message a friend or write a note to our parents or tell a teacher or coach how grateful we are for the support they give us and that we don't take them for granted.

A sincere and heartfelt thank you can say many things. It can say *I see you*. It can say *I see what you have done for me*. And it can say *I appreciate the kindness you have shown me. I am grateful for you.*

We must remember to be grateful for being alive and being who we are. Practicing gratitude helps us be mindful of what an amazing gift our life is. For one month, each day ask and answer three questions:

What am I grateful for in my life?

What one thing am I really grateful for today?

How can I show my gratitude today to someone else?

Have you heard?

"Gratitude is the greatest of virtues and the parent of all others."
Cicero ~Roman lawyer, statesman, orator, and philosopher

Why do you think he meant?

Light your path

Light your path with **Simplicity**. How do *you* define simplicity? How do you show it? Blaze a trail this way...

I am not distracted by the frantic frenzy of life. I am organized and prioritize my daily activities. I pay as much attention to getting rid of things as I do adding them. I avoid gossip and drama because they are a waste of energy. I focus on one thing at a time and do my best. I know that *less is more*, that quality is more important than quantity. I don't have to always be on-line or on my phone. I set aside time each day to slow down, unplug, relax, and maybe even do nothing.

Pathways to **simplicity** come from a power within you. For example, if you find that your friends are spreading a nasty rumor about someone on social media or at school, you ignore it and do not pass it along. Or if you are asked to join a bunch of school clubs or teams, you say "no" to some of them because you want to stay focused and not get spread too thin. Or if you seem to be rushed much of the time, and are late a lot, you streamline your schedule to slow things down.

Today come up with three things to stop doing to simplify life and make it less busy.

Have you heard?

"Life is really simple, but we insist on making it complicated." Confucius ~Chinese wisdom teacher and philosopher

What do you think he meant? Why do you think keeping things simple is so important?

Shine the light

The wise ones agree on the wisdom of simple things. It is often the small and simple things that matter most and make a big difference.

Some old-school wisdom that still makes sense today: Speak clearly. Look people in the eye. Say *please* and *thank you*. Wash your hands. Brush your teeth. Hand write notes of gratitude. Arrive early. Wear neat, clean clothes. Remember names. Keep your word. Do not gossip. Be helpful whenever you can. Avoid using too much profanity. Smile, say a warm *hello,* and be kind to each person you meet.

Remember to eat healthy, get enough sleep, and exercise each day. Above all else, make your bed every morning!

What small but important things can you start doing today?

Change your mind

Use a new mindset to better manage the day-to-day busyness of life.

Stop forcing things and acting with so much urgency and certainty.

Start being active but also at ease, and intentional but also relaxed.

Around the world

Tao

(pronounced *dow*)

Tao is a Chinese concept that means the way, path, or road of wisdom. The Tao is the natural order of the universe, the proper way of existence that is moral and enlightened, but impossible to define.

The Tao is a timeless and formless force governing the cosmos. It is paradoxical: it teaches us that less is more, to slow down, simplify, streamline, and strip away our beliefs to see the world more clearly.

Do you understand?[5]

A boy and a girl are standing at their bus stop, each with their calendar apps up on their phones. The girl says, "Okay, I can move ballet back an hour, reschedule yoga, and cancel my SAT prep class. You can shift your violin lesson and skip soccer practice. That way we can meet up at Starbucks on Thursday from 3:15-3:45pm. Sound like a plan?" The boy says, "Wait, you want a whole half-hour? Let's try for next month."

Can you relate to this story? What are some of the benefits of slowing things down?

Have you heard?

"Beware the barrenness of a busy life." Socrates ~Greek philosopher, ethicist, and teacher

What do you think he meant? Why do you think being less busy is more healthy?

Shine the light

Many years ago, a Zen master once said that enlightenment is to *chop wood and carry water*.

People who are joyful take joy in everyday ordinary things:

If you are hungry, enjoy eating.
If the grass is long, enjoy mowing it.
If you are playful, enjoy playing with friends.
If the floor is dirty, enjoy sweeping it.
If you are tired, enjoy sleeping.

How might you pay more attention to and more enjoy doing ordinary things each day?

Epigram I am

It is said that nothing is impossible,

But I do nothing every day!

Check your reality[6]

Have you noticed that when we keep things simple and stay present, the ordinary can become extraordinary?

A teacher is outside of school and sees five of his students coming from the market on bicycles. He asks, "Why are you riding your bicycles?"

One student says, "My bicycle is carrying groceries that I will take home to my parents later." And the teacher praises him.

Another student says, "I love to watch trees and fields pass by as I bike down the path." And the teacher praises him.

The third student says, "When I ride my bicycle, I can clear my mind from stress." And the teacher praises him.

The fourth says, "Riding my bike, I feel a freedom and harmony with the world." And the teacher praises him.

The last student says, "I ride my bicycle to ride my bicycle." The teacher then bows to her and says, "Now I am *your* student."

Do you realize that sometimes just doing what you are doing is all that needs to be done?

Have you heard?

"Life is not a problem to be solved, but a reality to be experienced."
Soren Kierkegaard ~Danish philosopher, poet, and theologian

What do you think he meant?

Haiku for you

Out in the orchard

I pick limes, lemons, oranges

Here is quiet peace

Shine the light

We affect others in many ways. This is called the *ripple effect* or *butterfly effect*. Both refer to a few principles that describe our world:

We all come from and are all made of the same stuff. Everything in the world is connected to everything else. Every single thing is attached to the rest of the world.

We can affect others by what we do or don't do. We can affect others by what we say or don't say. We can affect others by the positive or negative energy we radiate.

How do you affect the lives of other people each day? Are you interested in having a more positive affect on others? What might you start, stop, or continue doing?

True nature is

Your favorite book requires paper from wood pulp that comes from trees. Trees require earth, air, water, and sun to live and grow. Machines that make the book require electricity, that is generated from the earth, wind, sun, or water.

Making electricity to run the machines gives off carbon dioxide, some of which trees need to live and grow. As trees live and grow, they give off oxygen, which you breathe to live and grow, so that you can read **your favorite book**.

What do you think is meant by true nature? Do you see how everything is connected?

Around the world

Ubuntu

(pronounced *uu-**boon**-tuu*)

Ubuntu originates from southern Africa. It means that we are all connected as people, that our lives are intertwined by the spirit of being human. We are welcoming to, and responsible for, one another.

Ubuntu means kindness and warmth to both friends and strangers alike. We all belong to each other. When one of us suffers, we all suffer. When one of us rejoices, we all celebrate. We co-exist as one family.

Have you heard?

"If you wish to make an apple pie truly from scratch, you must first invent the universe." Carl Sagan ~American scientist, teacher, writer

"We are one thread in the web of life. Whatever we do to the web, we do to ourselves. All things are bound together; all things connect." Seattle ~Native American chief of Suquamish and Duwamish nations.

What do you think they meant?

Do you understand?

One day a young man's friend was trying out his new hoverboard on the sidewalk, got out of control, and veered into the street. A mom in his neighborhood had to swerve her car quickly to avoid running into him. Instead of hitting his friend, she hit a parked car.

She was okay, but the parked car was that of the young man's piano teacher, who was in the area giving a lesson. It was towed to a mechanic to get fixed. With his car at the shop, the teacher was not able to drive to the young man's house and cancelled the music lesson.

So the young man watched television instead, which put his sister in a foul mood since she hated his shows. As retribution, she told his parents about him calling her a bad name at school, which got him grounded for two weeks. All this because of a hoverboard mishap!

Have you noticed in your own life how people and events are connected in many ways?

Epigram I am

We might all be connected in the web of life,

but sometimes I feel like I'm just hanging-on by a thread!

Light your path

Light your path with **Discernment**. How do *you* define discernment? How do you show it? Blaze a trail this way…

I am careful in how I think and thoughtful in how I use my reasoning. I can distinguish facts from opinions, and am aware of the differences between facts, beliefs, and feelings. I show sound judgment without being judgmental. I am a good listener and observer. I analyze situations, recognize patterns, and gain insight from what I learn. I see how forces in the world try to condition how I think and what I believe. I understand there are both rational and emotional reasons for believing something or making a decision. I am intentional in using practical common sense to make sound decisions and good choices.

Pathways to **discernment** come from a power within you. For example, you are discerning when it comes to your friends. You are open to new friendships, and may have many types of friends, but are careful in choosing your close friends. You avoid being in a clique or having just one best friend. You are cautious about which friends you open-up to about your personal experiences and feelings. You don't share personal information on social media and keep your private life private. You can tell the difference between real friends who truly care about you from pretend friends who do not. You choose your close friends wisely. The quality of your path depends a lot on the quality of your friends.

Today pay attention to all the different choices you get to make and how and why you make them.

Have you heard?

"Most people do not listen with the intent to understand; they listen with the intent to reply. Seek first to understand, then to be understood." Stephen Covey ~American writer, educator, speaker, and business leader

Why do you think active listening is important to discernment? Why is discernment so important in our complicated world that is full of distractions?

Did you know?

You might feel you are less than or different from others.

You might feel separate, lonely, anxious, or that you don't belong.

You might feel you are uncomfortable in your own skin.

And did you know?

You are not alone in feeling this way.

These are natural and perfectly normal feelings.

Many young people have these feelings but try to cover them up.

And did you also know?

You don't need to cover them up or try to be someone you are not.

You don't even have to figure out why you feel this way.

Feel these normal feelings and then let them go.

Think about what these principles mean. How might they help you walk your path?

Shine the light

There is a big difference between guilt and shame. It has been said that we feel guilt for what we've done and shame for who we are.

Guilt is usually okay and can even be helpful: Guilt is "I *made* a mistake" or "I *did* a bad thing." We all make mistakes; we can take responsibility for them. We address our guilt through amends and apologies if we can and then move on. We do not allow others to make us feel guilty.

Shame is not okay and is very unhealthy: Shame is "I *am* a mistake" or "I *am* bad." No person is a mistake; we are all equal as human beings. We must be kind and gentle with ourselves, like we would with a friend who is struggling, and let shame go. We do not allow others to make us feel shame.

The researcher, speaker, and author Brené Brown has said, "What we don't need in the midst of a struggle is shame for being human."

When do you feel guilt or shame? How might you be more aware of the difference between them? Do you see how shame is harmful to you?

Light your path

Light your path with **Dignity**. How do *you* define dignity? How do you show it? Blaze a trail this way…

I am worthy of love and respect. I am inherently a good person. I treat myself and others with respect and care. I value what I believe, how I feel, and who I am. I show self-control in hard situations and poise when things get tough. I stay composed when I feel uncomfortable. I avoid acting impulsively and don't need to do everything I feel like doing. I don't cover up mistakes; I show integrity in owning and fixing them. In my heart I know what is right and follow my conscience.

Pathways to **dignity** come from a power within you. For example, you recognize that movies, websites, apps, music, and advertising often cheapen sexuality and promote risky sex. There is a lot of pressure to do senseless things like sexting or participate in careless sexual activity. But you know how important it is to make good, healthy decisions about your body and reputation. You do not hide from or fear your own gender, sexual orientation, or sexuality. You wait as long as you want before exploring sex, and are patient for the right time to share the gift of intimacy with another person. If others make fun of you for waiting, it has nothing to do with you; it is their own insecurity.

Today notice all the different ways that society conditions you to feel less-than worthy or unworthy.

Have you heard?

"Dignity is the belief in oneself, that one is worthy of the best. Nothing can dim the light that shines from within." Maya Angelou ~African-American poet, dancer, and singer

"Don't ever let another soul in the world tell you that you can't be exactly who you are." Lady Gaga ~American singer, songwriter, actor, and performance artist

What did they mean? Why do you think dignity is so important in walking your path?

Think about this

What is responsibility? There are many facets to it. How do you define responsibility? A practical definition is dependably meeting obligations or carrying out duties. Responsibilities often involve doing assigned tasks, projects, and activities that are within our power to complete in a reliable and diligent way.

There is also responsibility for one's decisions and actions. This is known as accountability. The decisions we make, and the actions we take, have consequences, some of which we may view as good while others we may view as bad. The key is to think through what might happen before we do something, so we can try to do the right thing.

It is important to remember that others don't know what is best for us and we don't know what is best for them. We are responsible to discern what is best for ourselves. We can seek help and listen to advice, believing that friends, family members, mentors, and teachers have our best interest in mind. But we are responsible for trusting ourselves.

There is more to responsibility than all of this, however. Wise sages and great leaders throughout history believed that responsibility is the power to shape and respond to life as we walk our path. Each of us has a responsibility to live a virtuous and purposeful life through ethical reason, careful judgment, and self-reflection. What does this mean?

Responsibility is the power to choose, to be intentional. We have the power to live our values and beliefs, learn and grow, do our best, change what we can, and actively participate in life. We have the power to be fully aware, and the responsibility to creatively use the full capacity of our minds.

What are you responsible for? How seriously do you take your responsibilities? What do you think is meant by responsibility as power?

Have you heard?

"You have the power over your mind, not outside events. Realize this and you will find inner strength." Marcus Aurelius ~Roman emperor, Stoic philosopher, and writer

"Man is ultimately self-determining. What he becomes — within the limits of endowment and environment — he has made out of himself." Victor Frankl ~Austrian pioneering psychologist, Holocaust survivor, and writer

"It is not what happens to you, but how you respond to it that matters." Epictetus ~Greek slave, Stoic philosopher, and teacher

What do you think they meant?

Pathways

Part 4

Topics

Equanimity ~ Impermanence ~ Middle way

Fearlessness ~ Physical fitness ~ Consciousness

Mindfulness ~ Meditation ~ Power ~ Balance

Healthy habits ~ Happiness ~ Hope

Do you understand?

There lived a dignified farmer who had worked his land for many years. One day his horse ran away. Hearing the news, his neighbors came to visit. "Such bad luck," they said with sympathy.

"Maybe," the farmer replied.

The next morning the horse returned, bringing with it three other wild horses. The farmer's neighbors were quick to respond. "How wonderful! What good luck," they exclaimed.

"Maybe," the farmer replied.

The following day, the farmer's son tried riding one of the untamed horses, was thrown, and broke his leg. The neighbors again came to offer their sympathy and said, "That's terrible! What bad luck."

"Maybe," the farmer replied.

The next day, military officials came to the village to draft all the young men into the army because a war was going on. Seeing that the farmer's son's leg was broken, they passed him by.

Many died in the war, but the farmer's son lived. The neighbors were very happy for the farmer, and said with sincere joy, "How great it was that your son could not fight!"

"Maybe," the farmer replied.

What does this story mean to you? Do you think the farmer was too indifferent to life? What was he passionate about?

Shine the light

Rumi was a Persian poet and Sufi mystic from ancient times who was very wise. Here is an adaptation of his poem, *The Guest House*:

This being human is like a guest house.
Every morning a new arrival.
A joy, a sadness, an anger
Come as unexpected visitors.
Welcome and entertain them all!
Treat each guest honorably.
He may be clearing the way
For some new delight.
Meet them at the door and invite them in.
Be grateful for whatever comes.
Each has been sent as a guide from beyond.

Why do you think he is suggesting we treat our feelings and emotions like guests?

Did you know?

Equanimity is the essence of spiritual wisdom. It means welcoming *every* situation, without judgment, as an opportunity to learn. It is a calm, composed, dignified attitude of appreciating *every* life experience.

How is equanimity related to other virtues, like humility, compassion, and discernment?

Around the world

Shenpa

(pronounced *shen-pah*)

Shenpa is a Buddhist term that originates from the Tibetan region of central Asia. It means "biting the hook" and refers to how we immediately react to things we don't like in a negative manner. Rather than react, we can reframe and let go (and *not* take the bait).

Shenpa reflects how we are easily "activated" by a person or situation, and how we react impulsively in an unhealthy way. For example, when someone wrongs us, we bite the hook of rage, and get angry at them. Rather than lash out, we can stay cool (and *not* take the bait).

Think about this

We can be careful of attaching ourselves to people, places, or things. We can love our family and friends, enjoy our home, our school, and other favorite places, like the museum, the mall, or the movie theater. We know these things come and go, like the seasons of the year.

When we get overly attached to something, we only hurt ourselves. When we pass judgment on someone, or blame someone, we only hurt ourselves. When we have big expectations and try to control things, we only hurt ourselves. **Remember that nothing is permanent.**

In our material world, the world of form, everything is changing. When we forget this law of the universe, we become attached. We cling to ideas. We crave certain experiences. We want people to stay the same. Then, when things change, we can get frustrated or angry.

So we need to be careful of becoming too attached. This does not mean we shouldn't love or be loyal to others. It does not mean we shouldn't help people we care about. It simply means nothing stays the same, and that's okay! As a law of the universe, there's no need to fear it.

Have you heard?

"Nothing is absolute. Everything changes, everything moves, every-thing evolves. Everything flies and goes away." Frida Kahlo ~Mexican artist and political activist

What do you think she meant?

Epigram I am

If nothing is permanent, and everything changes,

I keep wondering how this law of the universe always stays the same!

Did you know?

We are wired to be impulsive and reactive.

Our mind likes the roller coaster of emotional highs and lows.

We can practice the middle way to be more steady.

Think about what these principles mean. How might they help you walk your path?

Think about this

Walking *the middle way* is about letting go of attachments, accepting life on life's terms, being comfortable with uncertainty, maintaining a life in balance, and not taking yourself too seriously.

If you get caught up in thinking too much about something, like how much you want that new smartphone, **reframe**! Stop dwelling on it. Think about the nice things you have however small they might be.

If you get caught up in resenting a friend with whom you are very angry, **reframe**! Change your thought-process. Think about something you like about your friend however minor it might be.

If you get caught up in concerns about what's going on at school, or in your town, or around the world, **reframe**! Let the worries go. Keep things in perspective. Help-out if you can however limited it might be.

The middle way is the art of non-reaction and a mindset of calm humility. You can still address whatever bothers you, but also avoid drama, keep it simple, and stay cool.

What is the essence of the middle way? Why is it important to reframe at times to stay centered? How useful would it be to become skilled at reframing?

Have you heard?

"Sometimes the way is not clear; a calm and quiet mind can bring clarity." Melody Beattie ~American wellness teacher and writer

"Calm mind brings inner strength and self-confidence that is very important for good health." The Dalai Lama ~Tibetan and Buddhist spiritual leader

What did they mean? What does she mean by *the way* in the first quote?

Check your reality

Have you noticed that different types of fear are often behind how we perceive a situation and how we react to it?

When things get tough or we feel uneasy or are shocked by some-thing we didn't expect, we may feel that we want to *fight* or *flee* or *freeze*. These are natural reactions. Instead, with some awareness we can acknowledge our fear, say hello, not empower it, and go with the flow.

We must protect ourselves if we feel unsafe, if we are truly in danger. Some fear can be healthy and helpful. Usually, though, we have a choice to stay cool, calm, and not be impulsive or overreact. If we do not give our fear the power to control us, then it will stop.

Fear seems to be everywhere these days. Some people in positions of power promote fear on purpose. They use fear to disrupt progress. What are we so afraid of? The unknown. When fear of the unknown leads to hate and greed, that is when it is most destructive.

We can choose to not let doubts and fears get in the way of using our talents and pursuing our dreams. Karen Casey, a spiritual wisdom teacher, has written, "Life is full of dangers, risks, and challenges. We can choose to meet them fearfully or in a spirit of welcome."

There is a saying: **Fear came knocking. Faith answered the door. Nobody was there.** Remember most fear is not real. Most of the time we do not need to *fight* or *flee* or *freeze*. Things are often not what they seem. We can trust our own awareness and have faith in ourselves.

Do you see how it is often best to go with the flow and have faith?

Have you heard?

"Fear is the mind-killer." Frank Herbert ~American science fiction novelist, newspaper journalist, and ecology educator

What do you think he meant?

Haiku for you

Let go and let flow

The sun rises and it sets

Embrace this knowing

Think about this

Unless we are in real danger, what is the value of fear? Most of the time fear is just a trick that our mind plays on us. Right now, wherever we are, chances are there is nothing to fear. There is no need to be afraid. Some people say that FEAR stands for **F**alse **E**vidence **A**ppearing **R**eal.

There is no need to worry about who likes us or who does not, or if we are good at something or not, or about what might happen tomorrow. Most of the time we feel fear because our mind is "wired" to worry about things. But there's very little value in it. We simply don't have to worry so much! **The key is to keep things in perspective.**

Fear often comes down to two storylines in our mind: the fear of losing something that we think we have *or* the fear of not getting something that we think we need. When fear arises, we can try to remember this and see if our fear has to do with one or the other. It probably does.

If we fully experience the moment right now without worry about the future, we have little to be concerned about. Without knowing it, we constantly seek stability and control, even though they are illusions. A more natural state is to feel groundless: perplexed, bewildered, and mystified. Would you agree life can seem pretty surreal at times?

There is no need to fear uncertainty or doubt ourselves and our ability to handle what comes our way. Doubt is just another form of false fear. Remember, nothing is permanent. Everything is always changing. **Excitement comes from *not knowing* what is going to happen next!**

What do you think is meant by groundlessness being a *more natural state*?

Have you heard?

"When we look our deepest fear in the face, we find there is nothing there." Pema Chödrön ~American spiritual teacher and Buddhist nun

"This is the central illusion in life: that randomness is a bad thing." Nassim Taleb ~Lebanese American risk analyst, statistician, and writer

What do you think they meant? How do we struggle against uncertainty? Why do we?

Have you heard?

"The best weapon against stress is our ability to choose one thought over another." William James ~American pioneer in psychology, philosophy, and pragmatism

What do you think he meant?

Think about this

We create most stress ourselves from our own thoughts, behaviors, and actions. We get caught up in the hurry and worry of the day.

Stress is the mind and body's response to difficult situations, whether real or perceived. But stress does not always have to be a bad thing.

It is natural to feel stressed for an exam or a big game. Stay focused and use the stress to feel excited. **Stress can be a source of energy!**

It is easy to allow feelings of stress and anxiety to negatively affect us. Here are a few things we can do to reduce unhealthy stress:

Take long walks in nature.

Eat well and exercise regularly.

Make time for both rest and play.

Don't rush; leave early to arrive early.

Laugh a lot; don't take things so seriously.

Shine the light

Exercise is critical for good health. Physical fitness is proven to reduces stress and is key to healthy mind, body, and spirit.

Exercise should be a mix of aerobic, core strength, and flexibility. Good activities done safely, and with help if needed, are: stretching, light weight-lifting, biking, skating, running, hiking, kayaking, dancing, martial arts, yoga, pilates, tai chi, swimming, gymnastics, other sports.

We spend too much time inactive. At least one hour of moderate to vigorous physical activity every day is needed for our wellbeing.

What is your exercise program? Are you doing enough physical activity?

Shine the light

It has been said that serenity equals reality minus expectations.

Having too high of expectations for what *should* be, making too many assumptions about what *would* be, and believing too much in stories about what *could* be, can cause much disappointment in our lives. We can get frustrated, resentful, and even angry when we aim *should*, *would*, and *could* at ourselves or at others. Similar offenders are *must*, *ought*, *need to*, and *have to*.

We all have preferences and it is natural to want certain outcomes. We need to be careful, however, of attaching to our wants in unhealthy ways, and expecting too much. Disappointment and resentment come from the gap between how we think life is supposed to be and how it really is. The gap can be reduced by taking care in how we think about and use *could*, *would*, and *should*.

It's good to get real about expectations, assumptions, and beliefs.

How and how often do you use *could*, *would*, and *should*?

Did you know?

A very negative force in the world is resentment.

A resentment is a grudge against a person, place, or situation.

A resentment is a story your mind tells you for why you are angry.

And did you know?

A very positive force in the world is forgiveness.

When you don't take things personally, you can easily forgive.

Not taking things personally, and forgiving others, will set you free.

What do these principles mean to you? How are fear and resentment related? Why is forgiveness so important? What does it mean to be *set free*?

Have you heard?

"The practice of forgiveness is our most important contribution to the healing of the world." Marianne Williamson ~American spiritual teacher, author, and speaker

What do you think she meant? How does forgiveness heal?

Think about this

You are not your mind. You are not your body. You are not your thoughts or feelings. You are not your texts, snapchats, or hashtags. You are something much deeper, and it has no shape or form.

It is true your thoughts help create your life. There is great power in thought. The quality of how you think can affect the quality of your life. But the voice in your head is not who you are and not always very trustworthy. So who are you really? Who is your authentic self?

You are conscious life. You are spirit or soul which is only pure and good and free. Some call this consciousness. Some call it essence. Many believe your spirit or soul is eternal, that it exists forever.

What does it mean to become more conscious? How might spirit, soul, and consciousness be the same or different? Does it matter?

Have you heard?

"One's development is the passing from one state of consciousness to another." Alice Bailey ~American spiritual mystic, esoteric wisdom teacher, theosopher, and pioneer of the New Age movement

What do you think she meant? How does forgiveness heal?

Around the world

Dusha

(pronounced *duh-schah*)

Dusha originates from Russia and is used in many different contexts in the Russian language. It can be thought of as a synonym for person but has a mystical quality to it and really means soul or spirit.

Dusha suggests that a person and a soul are the same thing: that mind, body, and spirit are unified as one. A person is his or her spirit, full of depth and strength, vitality, kindness, and compassion.

True nature is

The French philosopher, René Descartes is considered the father of modern philosophy. In his most famous statement, he said:

"I think, therefore I am."

Another Frenchman, the existentialist philosopher Jean-Paul Sartre, disagreed with Descartes many years later. Sartre said:

"I know I'm thinking, therefore I am."

What is the difference between the beliefs of these two philosophers?

Have you heard?

"Rather than being your thoughts and emotions, be the awareness behind them. Observe your thoughts. Be the watcher." Eckhart Tolle ~German-Canadian spiritual writer and teacher

What do you think he meant?

Change your mind

Use a new mindset to better understand who you truly are.

Stop believing you are mind: thinking that you are your thinking.

Start believing you are awareness: your thinking about your thinking.

Epigram I am

True nature is the only thing I have that I never lost,

but have yet to find!

Think about this

The mind is both amazing and amusing! Each of us has a unique mix of memories, beliefs, ideas, and opinions. We perceive the world in different ways. **Unfortunately, our minds do not always serve us well.** We often see or hear or feel what our mind wants us to.

The mind can be thought of as an inner dialog, a conversation we constantly have with ourselves. Sometimes our mind makes up stories that are not true, and we believe them—stories about our self-image and self-identity: who we think we should be versus who we are.

Our mind wants us to stand out and be special, but also blend-in and be part of the crowd. It wants us to feel separate from and superior to others, but also fit-in and belong to a group. What stories does your mind tell you? How can you stay chill with all these mixed messages?

We can stop being so demanding of ourselves. We can stop being so critical of ourselves. We can look at each day not as a day to be perfect but as a day to learn something new. And we can let our minds wander and our thoughts flow without believing everything they suggest.

Observe how your mind works. Think about what you are thinking about. Your mind can come up with some crazy ideas. Don't take it too seriously. Laugh at it. And do not equate your thoughts to who you are. Speak kindly to yourself, and every now and then, ask:

Do I observe how my mind makes up stories?

Do I resist acting on every first thought?

Do I keep my inner dialog positive?

Do I smile at how my mind works?

True nature is

Sit in a comfortable chair and relax your body. Watch your thoughts. Think of your thoughts as a movie. See them fly across the screen of your mind. See how random and disconnected and funny they are.

Watch this movie of mental chatter for five minutes. See how thoughts come and go over and over. See how they feed on each other. See how entertaining your mind actually is. **Still think you are your mind?**

What do you think is meant by true nature?

Have you heard?

"Becoming awake involves seeing our own confusion more clearly."
Chögyam Trungpa ~Tibetan meditation master and Buddhist scholar,
teacher, and writer

What do you think he meant?

Think about this

Remember when you were very young and could play with your toys
for a long time without worrying or thinking about anything else?
Now that you are older, do you find you have a lot on your mind?
Does your mind feel cluttered and your thoughts scattered? Does the
chatter upstairs make it hard to concentrate when you need to?

Monkey mind is natural for most of us. It can be both amusing and
frustrating. What does it take to keep your mind more quiet and
focused? **It takes awareness and practice!** Relax and pay attention to
your breathing. Use imagination to observe your thoughts come and
go. In times when monkey mind is especially active, try to imagine:

Laying on a beach watching your thoughts float away on clouds.

Sitting near a stream watching your thoughts float by on leaves.

Thoughts leaving your head and catching fire as they fly to the sun.

Shine the light

**For many years a town elder was known to spend a few hours each
day in a river canyon cave chanting this verse:**

Thoughts come and thoughts go
Feelings come and feelings go
No beginning and no end
Again and again and again.

Why do you think this chant was helpful to her?

Shine the light

For thousands of years, people around the world have practiced meditation. Each day, people of all ages practice many different types and forms of this contemplative activity.

The positive effects of meditation on health and wellbeing are amazing. Meditation has been medically *proven* to help reduce stress, control anxiety, improve attention, enhance concentration, manage pain, improve sleep, and increase optimism and positive thinking.

Meditation reflects a variety of practices. It can be a quiet introspection, a calm self-reflection, a relaxed observation of time and space. It often involves sitting still and breathing deeply from the belly. It is a technique for opening one's mind and slowing one's thoughts.

Ancient masters believed the highest level of meditation is effortless: to rest in the present moment, relax in your natural state of mind, and experience your own beingness.

Are you willing to try meditation? Could you try it with a friend or teacher?

Check your reality

Have you ever wondered about the source of your personal power?

Energy cannot be created or destroyed, only channeled. If you give energy to other people, and what they say in the outer world, they will have power over you. If you give energy to trust and respect yourself in your inner world, you will have great power to light your own path.

Your inner world is your mind at work: the ability to let your thoughts flow while also guiding your thought-process to be useful. Do not turn the words of others into negative self-talk. Quiet the critical voice in your head. Mastering your inner dialog is true power.

Your consciousness determines the quality of your inner dialog. Elevate your consciousness and gain personal power three ways: contemplation, conversation, and creation. Practice observing yourself, talking with others, and expressing your thoughts and talents.

What is *inner world*? What do you give energy to? Is your inner dialog kind and helpful?

Do you understand?

A man who lived during the dark ages was arrested by a local baron and imprisoned deep in a dungeon run by a terrible jailer who wore a great key around his neck.

The man lived in the dungeon for many years, and each day, the door to his cell would burst open with food and water. He pleaded with the jailer to let him go, but the jailer would not respond.

The man became hopeless and wanted to die. He decided he would attack the jailer and hope the jailer would kill him in self-defense. To get ready, he examined the cell door.

He turned the handle and the door opened! There was no lock! So he left the cell, walked down the corridor, past the guards who paid no attention, and up the long stairs, out the front door of the prison.

The guards at the gate outside ignored him too, so he kept walking and went home a free man. It turned out he had been held captive not by stone and iron but by his own false beliefs.

What does this story mean to you? Can you think of a time when you thought you were locked into something, but it was because of your own mind?

Have you heard?

"There is only one cause of unhappiness in life: the false beliefs in your head." Anthony De Mello ~Indian Jesuit priest, psychotherapist, and spiritual teacher

What do you think he meant?

Check your reality

Have you noticed that your mind thinks in certain ways that tend to repeat themselves in patterns?

Not only does your mind play tricks on you, but your mind is also conditioned to think and view the world in certain ways. We are like computers since, whether we know it or not, we are programmed to repeat thought patterns that don't serve us very well. Consider:

We snap at a friend because we are angry about something else.

We believe we know what someone else is thinking or feeling or why they are doing something without asking them.

We use all-or-nothing thinking. Have you ever said something like "That coach is terrible; she has no idea what she is doing"?

We like to exaggerate and make things better or worse than they are.

We often label, generalize, or stereotype people. Have you ever said something like "Because he is Moslem he must hate Christians"?

We think our opinions are better than others. Have you ever said something like "He has no taste in music if he likes that group"?

We take credit for our success and blame others for our mistakes.

We may belittle others to feel better. Have you ever said something like "Can you believe she wore those clothes to school"?

We take something personally when it isn't personal, like feeling hurt when someone does not return a text, only to find that they forgot.

We ignore facts and clear evidence when they threaten our beliefs.

If you see yourself thinking or saying things like these, it means you are human! Being careful and aware of your mind is called being mindful. You can change how your mind works. You can start by always being kind and thoughtful when communicating with others.

Are you careful about what you say and how you say it? Do you practice loving-kindness when you speak and communicate?

Have you heard?

"Good habits formed in youth make all the difference." Aristotle ~Greek philosopher, scientist, and teacher

What do you think he meant?

Shine the light

Speech patterns reflect who we are. Richard Rohr, an American spiritual writer and wisdom teacher has suggested that:

Thoughts become words. Words become actions. Actions become habits. Habits become character. Character becomes destiny.

Our beliefs and values influence which thoughts become words and actions. Ultimately, our character reflects what we say and do.

What healthy habits do you want to start? What unhealthy habits do you want to stop?

Have you heard?

"Words are the voice of the heart." Confucius ~Chinese wisdom teacher and philosopher

What do you think he meant?

Around the world

Sawubona and **Sikhona**

(pronounced *sow-boh-nah and see-koh-nah*)

Sawubona is a greeting used by the Zulu of South Africa. It means "I see you." It reflects the privilege of being present with another person, being open and honest with them, and affirming their value.

The Zulu respond with Sikhona, which means "I am here." It reflects the willingness of the receiver to also be present and respectful, and fully participate in the moment both people are sharing together.

Have you heard?

"Listen with ears of tolerance. See through eyes of compassion. Speak with the language of love." Rumi ~Persian poet, teacher, and Sufi mystic

What do you think he meant?

Shine the light

There was once a Zen master who said:

"Do not seek the truth; just cease to have so many opinions."

In another account, he was heard to have said:

"Do not seek the truth; just cease to pass judgment on others."

What do you think he meant? Is he really saying the truth is not important?

Did you know?

Gossiping and spreading rumors are very unhealthy for you.

Judging, complaining, and making excuses are also very unhealthy.

The less you talk, the less you need to worry about what you say.

And did you know?

When you speak, ask yourself: Is it necessary?

When you speak, ask yourself: Is it kind?

When you speak, ask yourself: Is it true?

Why is right speech so important?

Epigram I am

I can resist the trap of certainty,

Except when I'm certain your opinion is wrong!

Think about this

Has someone ever said to you that it is important to be well-rounded? Another way of saying this is that it is healthy to live a balanced life, where our activities and experiences blend nicely together and are in harmony as a whole. What does this mean? And why does it matter?

To be well-rounded means to balance school, work, family, friends, sports, and other interests without much stress or fatigue. We are active, but don't overdo it, and take time to relax. There is a rhythm to daily life that feels good mentally, emotionally, and physically.

Sometimes, though, we may feel out-of-synch. We can become preoccupied with feelings of *not enough* or *needing more*. We forget the importance of balance in mind-body-spirit needed to function as an integrated self. Consider how life can become unbalanced. Do you:

Work or study so hard you don't have time for family or friends?

Spend your free time video gaming and don't get outdoors?

Stay attached to your phone all day and don't unplug?

Only play sports and don't get creative through art or music?

Have such a busy life that you don't eat or sleep well?

Go all the time and don't slow down and enjoy just being?

A balanced life can be thought of as a stable four-legged stool. The first leg is family and friends; the second leg is school and work; the third leg is creativity and play; and the fourth leg is self-care and service to others. Are you paying attention to all four legs?

Life can get out of balance. This is natural, but it doesn't have to stay that way. We can remind ourselves that life is about the quality, and not the quantity, of experiences. We can hit the pause button, reflect on our daily lives, and look for ways to flow, simplify, or streamline.

What can you stop, start, or continue to help keep your life in comfortable balance?

Shine the light

A wise trainer once said the most skilled helpers in life are:

Direct sunlight, clean water, clear air, daily exercise, frequent laughing, quiet rest, nutritious food, and an easygoing attitude.

Why do you think we often forget about the basics?

Do you understand?[7]

An old Native American chief of the Cherokee nation was teaching his grandson about life. "A fight is going on inside me," he said to the boy. "It is a terrible fight between two powerful wolves."

The chief continued, "One wolf is evil—he is angry, greedy, self-centered, dishonest, fearful, arrogant, and full of sorrow and misery. The other wolf is good—he is kind, peaceful, caring, honest, compassionate, generous, and full of gratitude and joy."

He then said to the boy, "The same fight is going on inside you, and in every person." The grandson thought about this and asked, "Which wolf will win?" The old chief replied, "The wolf you feed."

What does this story mean to you? What was the chief trying to teach his grandson?

Think about this

An evil wolf is prowling around, the wolf of drugs and alcohol. It is a wolf in sheep's clothing and can take over our lives. It is okay to take medication prescribed by a doctor or other healthcare professional. But if we decide to use other kinds of drugs or smoke or vape or abuse alcohol, it can easily bring us grief, pain, and suffering.

Drugs and alcohol can eat away at our health when abused. They numb our senses and give us a false sense of relief. They can destroy who we are and cause us to act like someone we are not. Rather than use drugs or alcohol, we can do healthy things like exploring nature, playing music or sports, exercising, and volunteering.

There are other evil wolves prowling around too, the wolves of social media, pornography, and video games. They offer instant gratification and seem harmless. But they can easily become harmful obsessions that distract us from doing meaningful things like spending time developing good friendships and expressing ourselves creatively.

Are you feeding any of these wolves? Are you preoccupied with any of them? Are you interested in replacing them with healthier activities—with the good wolves?

Shine the light

What is happiness? Happiness is a very positive feeling and emotion. Each of us probably has a different definition of happiness.

Consider this definition as you think about your own: Happiness **is** how kind and caring you are with yourself, how kind and generous you are with friends, how kind and friendly you are with others, and how active you are in learning from new experiences.

Happiness doesn't come from the outside. It doesn't come from praise or pleasure. It's not feeling great all the time, having a lot of money or material things, or avoiding pain or negative stuff in the world.

Happiness comes from the inside. It is an inner state that comes and goes, and is generated by how we think and what we do each day. It is activated from kindness, generosity, friendliness, and creativity.

Young people who are happy a lot of the time spend less time gaming and watching television, and spend more time studying, being with family and friends, and pursuing interests that stretch their skills.

Consider these keys to being happy more often: Stretch yourself to accomplish something worthwhile. Help other people in meaningful ways. Express yourself creatively in meaningful ways. Show your gratitude in meaningful ways.

While genetics and circumstances can affect our happiness, much of happiness comes from our choices, healthy habits, and state of mind.

How might you feel more happy? What is meant by *worthwhile* and in *meaningful ways*?

Have you heard?

"The happiness of your life depends upon the quality of your thoughts." Marcus Aurelius ~Roman emperor and Stoic philosopher

"Happiness is when what you think, what you say, and what you do are in perfect harmony." Mahatma Gandhi ~Indian human rights leader and activist

What did they mean? Is there a difference between happiness and joy?

Do you understand?[8]

There was once a good-natured monk, called a *lama* in his native land. Some called him the Jolly Lama. Walking in the woods, he came to a fallen tree. He tried to jump over it and fell face-first in the mud.

He laughed and got up and tried it a second time, only to fall face-first in the mud again. He tried and failed several more times and laughed even harder every time he fell in the mud.

Finally, he made it over only to fall into the mud on the other side. Laughing so hard he could barely breathe, he patted the log as if it was a lifelong friend and continued his walk in the woods.

What does this story mean to you?

Have you heard?

"Laughter is the language of the soul." Pablo Neruda ~Chilean poet and political activist

"Life is too important to be taken seriously." Oscar Wilde ~Irish poet, playwright, novelist, and aesthetic

"Laughter keeps you healthy. You can survive by seeing the humor in everything." Bel Kaufman ~American teacher and writer

What do you think they meant? Why is it good to laugh at the world and yourself?

Did you know?

To laugh is to celebrate the wonders of life with someone else.

Laughter is the best way to share your joy with others.

To laugh a lot is to live a longer happier life.

Think about what these principles mean. Are you ready to laugh more?

Haiku for you

I observe my thoughts

Hoping the sun, wind, and clouds

Will laugh well with me

Think about this

It is good to be clear about what you want. It is just fine to want to have or achieve certain things. Maybe you want a new video game or pair of shoes. Maybe you want to be the starting goalkeeper or improve at playing the guitar. Maybe you want that great job after school.

Envision what you want and envision receiving it. If you stay focused and positive, work hard, and do your best, you can achieve many things. At the same time, never feel they are owed to you. Be grateful and content with who you are and what you have.

Your imagination, intention, and attitude are a big part of the recipe for success in life. Eckhart Tolle, the spiritual wisdom teacher, said: "You attract and manifest whatever corresponds to your inner state." In other words, like attracts like: think, ask, believe, act, and receive.

This has often been called the **Law of Attraction**. Here is an affirmation to attract into your life the things you want. Thinking and then saying out loud something like this each day will help "pull the weeds and plant the seeds" in your mind to realize what you can imagine:

I am clear about what I want.

I sense my oneness with all life.

I visualize receiving what I want.

I let go of all sense of limitation.

I will work hard for what I want

I am open to a life of abundance.

Have you heard?

"What you think you become. What you feel you attract. What you imagine you create." Siddhartha Gautama ~the Buddha, Indian mystic and founder of Buddhism

"The best way to predict your future is to create it." Abraham Lincoln ~American statesman and president

How have you experienced the law of attraction in your life? What does it mean to live life positively and intentionally?

Shine the light

What is hope? Hope is about the future you wish to experience. You can create hope in your life in these ways:

Believe life is full of possibilities — you have the power to pursue them. Set a few goals or aspirations — take aim at a direction you want to go. Determine specific actions for achieving those goals — then get active. Stay flexible — there is more than one way to achieve your goals. Embrace surprises as neither good or bad — then learn from them. Visualize success — see the future you want, be positive, and have faith.

Hope is a choice: we can choose to feel hopeful. Hope is a process: we can then take action. And hope is a mindset: we can be optimistic.

How might you think differently about hope? What do persistence and resilience have to do with hope? What does it mean to adapt and embrace surprises?

Have you heard?

"You are capable at any time of doing what you dream of." Paulo Coelho ~Brazilian lyricist, novelist, and spiritual teacher

"Within you is the strength, patience, passion to change the world." Harriet Tubman ~African-American abolitionist and humanitarian

"Hope is a passion for the possible." Soren Kierkegaard ~Danish philosopher, poet, and theologian

What do you think they meant?

Change your mind

Use a new mindset to think positively about this day and the future.

Stop using this frame: You are the victim of your situation.

Start using this frame: You are the hero of your story.

Think about this

Another law related to the Law of Attraction is the **Law of Reflection**. This law says that what you are to the world, it will be back to you. How you experience the world can be thought of as a reflection, as if from a mirror, of how the world experiences you. The attitude that you show the world influences how others respond to you.

If you respect yourself, and respect others, then they will respect you in return. If you are positive, other people will react to you in positive ways, and positive things in general will happen. If you are negative, the world will be a more negative place too. The key is to be intentional about how you "show up" in your everyday activities.

How have you experienced the law of reflection in your life?

Have you heard?

"Life will be to you what you are to it." Ernest Holmes ~American spiritual teacher, writer, and pioneer of the New Thought movement

"You do not attract what you want. You attract what you are." Wayne Dyer ~American spiritual teacher, motivational speaker, and writer

What do you think he meant?

Around the world

Karma and **Kifarah**

(pronounced **kahr-muh** and kee-far-ah)

Karma is a Sanskrit term that originates from ancient India. It means action, word, or deed. It reflects cause and effect, and a key principle of life: that one's intent and actions influence his or her future.

Some say that karma is continually getting the teachings we need to open our heart. Pema Chödrön, the spiritual wisdom teacher, has said, "Nothing goes away until it has taught us what we need to know."

In the Islamic tradition, Kifarah is similar and means that what you give, you will get back. In other words, do good things and good will eventually come to you. If you do bad things, you will struggle in life.

Did you know?

Life often feels unfair.

There are many injustices in this world.

Things often seem like they don't go our way.

And did you know?

Expecting fairness and justice can be very hard on you.

It is easy to become too attached to how things should be.

At times we can fall into the trap of feeling like a victim.

And did you also know?

Each of us has a right to be treated with respect and dignity.

Most everything else in life is not owed to us at all.

We have the right to work hard for what we want and what is right.

What do these teachings mean to you? How do you define what you want and what is right? How can you make sure these are healthy things?

Epigram I am

I know that I am a human being,

But sometimes I feel more like a human doing!

Have you heard?

"The only obligation which I have a right to assume, is to do at any time what I think is right." Henry David Thoreau ~American essayist, poet, philosopher, and naturalist

"The effective person puts more attention on doing the right things rather than doing things right." Peter Drucker ~Austrian-American business consultant, educator, and founder of modern management.

"It is time to start something new and trust the magic of beginnings." Meister Eckhart ~German theologian, monk, philosopher, and mystic

What did they mean? Are you willing to work hard for what you want and what is right?

Pathways

Part 5

Topics

States of mind ~ Faith ~ God

Religion ~ Reason and spirituality

Do you understand?

A long time ago, there once was a carpenter and a prince who met on a road. Both were walking and happened to cross paths.

The carpenter, named Jes, had been walking his path for years, and had come far from the west. The prince, named Sid, had also been walking his path for years, and had come far from the east.

Both had traveled a great distance, had met many people, and had overcome many obstacles. They greeted each other humbly, kindly, and warmly, appreciating the opportunity to stop for a while and rest and talk and have a drink of water.

After introducing themselves, they asked each other why the other was walking so far and where he was going.

Jes said, "I was told by a wise man when I was very young that one day I would change the world if I walked my path to share kindness and love with others." Then Sid said, "I too was told by a wise man when I was very young that one day I would change the world if I walked my path to share wisdom and insight with others."

Both Jes and Sid were somewhat intrigued by this coincidence and became more curious about the other. They asked each other how he had gained this important insight to help others.

After a slight pause, Sid said, "I wandered for several years learning as much as I could about the world until I sat under a tree for over forty days, and through much meditation, felt the spirit of life, love, and compassion enter my body."

Very surprised again at this coincidence, Jes replied, "I too wandered for several years learning as much as I could about the world until, after over forty days in the harsh wilderness, and through much prayer, felt the spirit of life, love, and compassion enter my body."

By this time, they were amazed at their similarities and good fortune and were very grateful to have met the other.

Jes then asked Sid, "Why would a prince walk such a path?" And Sid said, "It is true that I am called a prince, but that is not who I really am; rather, I am the spirit of the world that can help end suffering."

(continued on next page)

In return, Sid asked Jes, "Why would a carpenter walk such a path?" And Jes said, "It is true that I am called a carpenter, but that is not who I really am; rather, I too am the spirit of the world that can help heal the sick and feed the poor."

Both men became very quiet and thoughtful at this point and began to wonder if there was a reason that their paths had crossed.

Then Sid asked Jes if there was intolerance and hatred in the lands that he had walked. And Jes responded by saying that there was. Then Jes asked Sid the same question, and Sid responded that there was.

Then Jes said, "We should love our enemies as ourselves." And Sid agreed, then he said, "There are no real enemies, just people who are suffering." And Jes agreed as well.

Sid went on to say, "In my travels, I have tried to teach important values, called precepts, such as: one should refrain from taking life, one should refrain from stealing, and one should refrain from lying. This is the path to Nirvana."

Once again, more amazed than ever, Jes said, "In my travels, I have also tried to teach important values, called commandments, such as: you shall not kill, you shall not steal, and you shall not bear false witness. This is the path to Heaven."

Then both men shared that they were often misunderstood about these ideas, and that Nirvana and Heaven were not necessarily *destinations*, but were more like *states of mind* to be experienced when walking one's path with courage, humility, and kindness.

They became quiet again, realizing that there was, indeed, a reason that their paths had crossed.

Sid said he thought they could learn a lot from each other. Jes agreed and said he was thinking the same thing. Then they sat and rested a while, breathing fully and deeply, and enjoyed the warmth of the sun, the songs of birds, and the fragrance of flowers.

Breaking the spell, Jes asked, "What causes people to suffer so much?" With the sparkle of insight in his eyes, Sid responded, "It is their fear of impermanence and the unhealthy attachment they have to people, places, and things." And Jes thanked him for his wisdom.

(continued on next page)

Then Sid asked in return, "What causes people to suffer so much?" Now with his own sparkle, Jes responded, "It is their fear of the unknown and the lack of understanding that we are all connected as children of a divine presence." And Sid thanked him for his wisdom.

They talked well into the evening, laughing and singing, and learning from each other, grateful for their mutual kindness and openness to each other's views and ideas, some of which were similar and some of which were different.

Finally, Sid said, "I've had a vision that I will be called the Awakened One and that my teachings will help many people detach from and transcend the causes of their pain."

And Jes said, "I too have had a vision that I will be called the Anointed One and that my teachings will help many people embrace and overcome the causes of their fear."

After a modest meal of bread, cheese, berries, and water, they fell asleep by their campfire and slept soundly under the shining stars.

The next morning, they were gone, with no trace they had ever been there, and to this day no one can really be sure if they ever actually met. But many believe that each man went on walking his path to help many others connect with the divine spirit deep inside each of us.

Who were these men and what does their story mean to you? What did they mean that Nirvana and Heaven are *not necessarily destinations but states of mind?*

Shine the light

Practice breathing deeply and think about the natural rhythms of our world. Think about how these things come and go:

The cycles of the seasons ...

The positioning of the stars ...

The currents of streams and rivers ...

The ebbs and flows of the tides ...

The tempo of the wind ...

The cadence of storm clouds ...

The phases of the moon ...

What is the rhythm of your own life? Is it serene or hectic? Is it tranquil or wild? Would you like life to have more of a rhythm? How would you do that?

Have you heard?

"Faith is the warmth underneath the motion of life." Manly Hall ~American esoteric and spiritual wisdom scholar, historian, and writer

What do you think he meant?

Do you understand?

A young man was worrying about the future and felt he did not know how to have faith, so he went to a wise deacon for advice. He asked, "How do I get more faith?" The deacon responded, "My son, faith is not something you find; it is something you receive."

The young man was a little confused by this, so he then asked, "Well, how do I receive it?" The deacon smiled and said, "That's simple but not always easy. You receive faith through gratitude." Again, he was surprised and confused by the deacon's response.

The young man had been unhappy with his life, so he asked, "Well, how much gratitude are we talking about?" The deacon laughed and said, "Gratitude for everything! An appreciation for all there is: your life, your friends, your family, and the whole world around you."

What do you think he meant? Why do you think faith comes from gratitude? Is this easy?

Think about this

Many people around the world believe that god is a supreme being who is all-knowing, all-powerful, and all-present. They share the belief that there is a divine presence "out there" that is conscious and greater than us. For thousands of years, people have called this being, or force, different names, such as God, Lord, Allah, Almighty, Creator, Shiva, Great Spirit, Universal Intelligence, Higher Power, and many others.

What does your family believe? This is important, but it is *your* choice how you define or believe in a power considered to be god.

Many people around the world also participate in a religion. Most religions include certain beliefs, rituals, and moral codes that describe what it means to live a good life. There are many great religions, or "faiths" on earth, such as Christianity, Islam, Judaism, Hinduism, and Buddhism. They are different in many ways but are also based on many similar ancient wisdom teachings. These teachings are recorded in the great spiritual writings such as the Tao Te Ching, the Vedas, the Upanishads, the Sutras, the Koran, the Torah, and the Bible.

What does your family believe and practice? This is very important, but it is *your choice* whether to practice a certain religion or faith.

What is meant by the "ancient wisdom teachings?" They are the values and virtues shared by spiritual people through the ages. Here is the great secret: regardless of their religion, time in history, or country of origin, the ancient wisdom teachers believed many of the same things! They believed almost universally in the sacredness of life and the dignity of the individual. And most of them agree on this:

Have no fear. There is a power greater than us. Our connection to this power and to each other is founded in love and compassion for all.

What do you believe and why? Are you still forming your own beliefs?

Have you heard?

"There should be no discrimination against languages people speak, skin color, or religion." Malala Yousafzai ~Pakistani humanitarian, activist, and survivor of terrorism

What do you think she meant?

Shine the light

Reinhold Niebuhr was an American ethicist and theologian. Here is part of a prayer he wrote that is used around the world every day:

God, grant me the serenity
To accept the things I cannot change,
The courage to change the things I can,
And the wisdom to know the difference.

This prayer is really a conversation with a higher power to help walk the middle way and live life freely without resistance to the now.

Francis of Assisi was a sainted Italian Catholic friar, leader, and preacher. Here is part of a prayer often attributed to him:

Lord, make me a channel of thy peace.
That where there is hatred, I may bring love.
That where there is despair, I may bring hope.
That where there is sadness, I may bring joy.

This prayer is also a conversation with a higher power to remember the purpose of life is to develop one's divine true self and help others.

What do these prayers mean to you? Do they have anything in common? Why do you think so many people find them so wise, spiritual, and inspiring?

Do you understand?

A young woman, who was very logical and a good math and science student, was struggling with spirituality, so she went to a wise leader in the community for help. She asked, "What does it mean to be spiritual or religious, and have faith, when you believe in science?"

The minister thought for a while and then responded, "What a great question! First of all, I'm not sure about the difference between religion and spirituality. Maybe it doesn't matter very much. For me, spirituality is about waking up — waking up to the reality of right now, to live in harmony with this reality, and not sleepwalk through life."

He went on, "It has taken me years to explore the mystery of faith. My faith is based on three principles: belief in a power greater than me; grateful acceptance of what is; and, trust that I'm in good hands. For me, it is wonderful how science, reason, and faith coexist to help understand the complexity of the world and this thing called life."

She wanted to know a lot more about what he meant, especially the part about waking up and not sleepwalking, but before she could ask more questions, the minister smiled and said, "It will be a great gift for you to explore these things on your own journey."

Do you think faith is a mindset or something more? How can science and faith coexist? In the last sentence, what is the minister suggesting to the young woman?

Have you heard?

"All religions, arts, and sciences are branches of the same tree. The more I study science the more I believe in God." Albert Einstein ~German-American physicist and philosopher

What do you think he meant?

Change your mind

A new mindset for how spirit and science, faith and reason converge.

Stop believing they represent rival ideas in conflict with one another.

Start seeing how they are complementary and connected to each other.

Shine the light

The Bahai faith emphasizes the inherent worth of all religions and the unity and equality of all people. This religion began in the Middle East in the mid-1800s and now has millions of members worldwide. Bahai teachings affirm the goals of a world unified in peace, the elimination of all prejudice, the harmony of religion and science, and the shared prosperity of all nations, races, and creeds.

The Unitarian Universalism religion emphasizes truth, meaning, and spiritual growth. This faith originated from progressive Christian congregations in New England in the early 1800s. Today, millions of members worldwide draw inspiration from all major religions and believe in the inherent dignity of every person and a world community focused on peace, intellectual freedom, and justice.

Why do you think so many people around the world practice "non-traditional" faiths?

Have you heard?

"I love you when you bow in your mosque, kneel in your temple, and pray in your church. For you and I are children of one religion, and it is the spirit." Kahlil Gibran ~Lebanese-American poet, essayist, and philosopher

What do you think he meant?

Pathways

Part 6

Topics

Adventure ~ Culture ~ Creation

Energy ~ Existence ~ Cosmos ~ Circle of life

Ecology ~ Environment ~ Community

Service ~ Helpfulness ~ Awareness

Success ~ Power ~ Essence

Shine the light

Walt Whitman was an American poet. Here are a few excerpts from an epic poem he wrote called *Song of the Open Road*:

Afoot and light hearted, I take to the open road, healthy, free, the world before me, the path leading wherever I choose.

To know the universe itself as a road, as many roads, as roads for traveling souls. Forever alive. Forever forward.

What do you think he meant?

Have you heard?

"Life is an unfoldment, and the further we travel, the more truth we can comprehend." Hypatia ~Greek-Alexandrian astronomer, scholar, librarian, and teacher

What do you think she meant?

Epigram I am

Whenever I see myself walking on the open road,

there's always a sign on the roadside that says, "Detour Ahead!"

True nature is

We are one world. Visit other cultures when you can. In the meantime, learn about them from their poetry, novels, art, music, films, and maps.

Explore the values and beliefs of other cultures. Learn about what is important to people in other countries around the world.

Explore the origins of other cultures. Learn about the history, geography, ethnicities, and language of people from other countries.

Explore the traditions of other cultures. Learn about the family rituals and spiritual practices of people in other countries.

Explore the ways of living of other cultures. Learn about how people live, work, go to school, and spend time with friends.

How might you start learning more about other cultures and traditions?

Did you know?

Every culture has its own creation story, or myth, about the beginning of the universe, the world, nature, and human beings.

These myths have much in common. With deities, magical creatures, and heroic men and women, they are very symbolic in nature and represent the beliefs and values of early civilizations.

They tell a story about how the cosmos formed from chaos into order, usually involving both natural and supernatural energy.

What do you think is meant by *natural* and *supernatural* energy?

Around the world

Mana

(pronounced *mah-nah*)

Mana is a term that is central to the Polynesian culture of many Pacific islands. Originally meant as a powerful force of nature, it translates as a supernatural energy in both animate and inanimate objects.

To have *mana* can mean many things such as influence, authority, or ability. In some cultures, most commonly, it means a sacred spiritual energy and healing power that can be gained or lost by one's actions.

Think about this

Our universe has been described as a cosmic dance of energy. As scientists have learned more about atomic particles, the building blocks of all that exists, we now know **everything is made of energy**. Everything in our world and out among the stars, is made of pure energy that we cannot see, smell, hear, or taste. But we can often feel it. Think about the energy you feel at a concert or on a first date.

We've learned strange things about the nature of matter and energy. At the quantum level, particles seem to exist only in relation to their observer. The act of observation itself affects what is observed. Some particles can also be so closely linked that they share the same existence, called entanglement. No matter how far apart they get, whatever happens to one particle will instantly happen to the other.

Energy is thus relational in nature. Each of us has an energy field that affects the energy field of the whole. Think about the energy you feel around a friend who is angry versus a friend who is happy. Our thoughts and behaviors create an energy field that can have a positive or negative charge, or vibration. There are "good" vibes and there are "bad" vibes. This is the dynamic energy field of our world.

Some believe that love has the highest vibrational frequency in the universe, and through thoughts and actions of loving-kindness, we can realize a sort of harmonic resonance and help create a unified future. If everything in our universe is energy, and if each of us affects this energy field, then we can affect the world for better or for worse. We all swim in the same ocean of energy together. **We are all connected!**

Why is positive energy so important? What is your own energy field like? What's your frequency? How might you want to change it?

Have you heard?

"If you want to find the secrets of the universe, think in terms of energy, frequency, and vibration." Nikola Tesla ~Serbian-American engineer, inventor, and futurist

What do you think he meant?

Did you know?

The energy field of our world is really a field of potentiality where just about anything is possible. It might be considered a field of dreams!

The energy from your thoughts, decisions, and actions reverberate in time and space and create your energy signature and your life.

Your energy links to the energy field of the cosmos, the network of existence. Your consciousness is an engine helping to power the world!

What do these principles mean to you? How might they help you walk your path?

Have you heard?

"We are in the universe and the universe is in us. We are all made of the same stardust." Neil deGrasse Tyson ~American astrophysicist, science educator, speaker, and writer

"The universe is a single living organism animated by a divine order and intelligence." Liz Greene ~British astrologer and psychologist

What do you think they meant?

Around the world

Qi

(pronounced *chee*)

Qi is a term used in Chinese, Korean, Vietnamese, Japanese traditions. It translates as breath, life force, or vital energy. It is the central idea in traditional Asian medicine, healing, contemplation, and martial arts.

Qi is the universal energy that makes up and flows through all things. It is the cosmic energy that is in everything, including us. It is the pulse of the universe that gives each of us health, vitality, and life.

Think about this

What is reality? What is existence? Questions about true nature have been pondered by many people for thousands of years.

There is the **physical** nature of a thing, such as a rock, an apple, a tree, an ocean, or a human being, and the tangible qualities they possess.

Do each of these things *exist* in the same kind of way? What is the cause and purpose of each object? What is its essence? Can we really know the full nature of something from its material form?

Many believe there is also a **metaphysical** nature of a thing, something beyond the physical, beyond our ability to perceive it using our senses.

Is it some form of spirit or energy or consciousness? Does it come from a divine power? Can we really know the full nature of reality, or is the reality we perceive just a mental model of our mind?

What do you think? Would you like to explore these big questions further?

Check your reality

Have you ever noticed that things are not always what they seem, and that people can see or experience the same event differently?

Imagine you and a friend travel on separate spaceships in different directions to explore the cosmos at high speeds across great distances. Even when using precise tools of measurement, you and your friend will not always agree on the distance between objects, the amount of time between events, or the sequence of those events.

Einstein's Relativity showed that time, space, and motion, and thus location and distance, are relative based on our frame of reference. As we go faster, time slows down. As gravity gets weaker, time speeds up. Distances can shorten or lengthen as well. All of this is true here on earth as well, we just can't perceive it using our own senses.

The speed of light is the only thing that is constant to all observers everywhere. Light moves so fast that it experiences no time at all! Three-dimensions are not sufficient to explain all of this strangeness! In fact, reality is best described using a four-dimensional model called spacetime, which represents the true geometry of causality.

What does all this mean to you with respect to your perception and the nature of reality?

Shine the light

Find a deep space image from a telescope. For two minutes look at it closely. In a way, you are now stargazing, which can be a very spiritual experience. What do you see?

Notice you are looking across unimaginable distances. Recognize you are looking back in time. Because of light's speed limit, looking into the distance is the same as looking into the past. The farther light has traveled to our eye the older it is.

Now consider we can only see about five percent of all that exists and don't know what the other ninety-five percent of the universe is made of! We call it dark matter and dark energy.

Are you aware of the incredible mystery of the cosmos? How does this make you feel? We often *zoom-in* to understand the nature of our minds and how we think. We can also *zoom-out* to understand the nature of our universe and how it works.

Breathe deeply and stargaze some more. The capacity of your mind grows with the scope of your view. To better comprehend the cosmos is to better comprehend ourselves.

What does it mean *to better comprehend ourselves*?

Have you heard?

"I have loved the stars too fondly to be fearful of the night." Galileo Galilei ~Italian pioneer of physics, mathematics, and astronomy

What do you think he meant?

Haiku for you

Bright Venus at night

Reflects on the dark water

Offering her hand

Do you understand?

You may have heard of the *circle of life*—that we come into this life through birth, made from the stuff of the universe, and leave it through death, our bodies returning to the stuff from which we were made. Or maybe you've heard of the *cycle of life*—that we are born, we live, and we die. Death is a fact of life; it is just as much a part of life as is birth.

There is an old story about a king who believed that the day of one's death is better than the day of one's birth. He believed that when a person is born, we should be happy but not rejoice for we don't yet know what kind of person the newborn will be, and that when a person dies, we should rejoice for a life well-lived.

A great challenge in life is to not fear death, but to understand it as a natural transition of our spirit into another state, just like birth is a transition, too. It is hard to think about this when we are young, but never too early to realize the more we live an active, productive, and spiritual life, the less we will worry about what happens when we die.

Does it make sense to think of death as a natural part of life? How do you view death?

Have you heard?

"People who live deeply have no fear of death." Anaïs Nin ~French-American diarist, essayist, and novelist

What do you think they meant?

Around the world

Enso and Yin-Yang

(pronounced *en-zo* and *yin-yang*)

Enso is a Japanese word that means circle. It is a symbol that is usually hand-drawn, either as a closed circle to represent perfection, or as a circle with a small opening to represent imperfection. An enso is often used to symbolize enlightenment and the simple elegance of reality.

Yin and yang are Chinese symbols that combine into a circle and reflect how seemingly opposed forces in the universe are actually interrelated, complementary, and in balance. Everything in the world has both yin and yang qualities. For example, dark cannot exist without light.

Shine the light

Native Americans believed in cycles of life. Black Elk was a spiritual leader and medicine man of the Oglala Lakota nation who said:

The power of the world always works in circles. The seasons form a great circle and always come back again to where they were. The life of a person is a circle, from childhood to childhood. And so it is in everything where the sacred power moves.

Why do you think circles are so sacred and spiritual?

Native Americans have rich spiritual traditions focused on the land. Reflect on this adaptation of a Native American prayer:

Great Spirit give us hearts to never take from creation's beauty more than we give or what we cannot use. Great Spirit, whose dry and depleted lands thirst, help us find the way to refresh them. Great Spirit, whose waters are choked with debris and pollution, help us find the way to cleanse them. Great Spirit, whose creatures are being destroyed, help us find a way to replenish them. Great Spirit, whose gifts to us are lost in selfishness and corruption, help us find the way to restore our humanity.

What or who do you think the Great Spirit is? Why is this prayer so important today?

Have you heard?

"You are not carrying the world on your shoulder. It is good to remember that the world is carrying you." Vandana Shiva ~Indian environmentalist and activist

"It is the little things that people do. That is what makes the difference. My little thing is planting trees." Wangari Maathai ~Kenyan environmentalist, writer, and teacher

What do you think they meant?

Think about this

We all come from the cradle of civilization in the heart of Africa. Humans migrated thousands of years ago to explore the world. Along the way, we developed different languages, traditions, religions, and physical features. We became tribal and started to believe that our differences defined us instead of our commonalities and shared origins and ancestry. We separated from each other and built walls.

When we walk our path, we can't do it alone. We must work together to ensure that our world is a healthy and prosperous place for the long-term. To do this, we can be curious about where we live to learn more about its natural history and human heritage. We are all responsible to take good care of our land, water, and air.

We are all tethered to the same ground, moored in the same sea, and blanketed by the same sky. We all share the same past and will participate in the same future. And we are all dependent on the resources our planet provides. A Native American proverb helps to remind and inspire us: **Treat the earth well. It was not given to you by your parents. It was loaned to you by your children.**

Now is the time to unite and preserve and improve the natural habitats and ecosystems — the ecology — of the world we share. We can better cooperate to help make our communities more safe, clean, sustainable, and abundant places to live for everyone. As Margaret Wheatley has written, "There is no power for change greater than a community discovering what it cares about." Take a moment and think about how important the following things are to you:

Contributing to the community ...

Conserving natural resources ...

Protecting the environment ...

Offsetting carbon emissions ...

Living in peace and harmony ...

Change your mind

Use a new mindset to collaborate with people in your community.

Stop focusing on how we are different and what we disagree about.

Start finding out what we have in common and what we agree on.

Around the world

Gaia

(pronounced *guy-uh*)

Named after a goddess in Greek mythology, Gaia refers to the earth as a single magnificent ecosystem in dynamic equilibrium. All lifeforms are part of a single living and evolving planetary being. Each lifeform therefore is equally important, and all must coexist to flourish.

Living organisms interact with their surroundings to form a complex, synergistic, and self-regulating system, called Gaia, which includes the biosphere, geosphere, hydrosphere, and atmosphere. Thus, the natural world requires a balance that is now at risk due to the human species.

Do you understand?[9]

A long time ago, an Aztec father told a story to his daughter in what is now Mexico. He started the story by describing how there was once a great fire in the forests that covered the earth at the time. People and animals had started to run for their lives to escape the fire.

Tecolotl, an owl, noticed a small bird hurrying back and forth between a nearby river and the fire. It was Quetzaltotatl, a quetzal bird, who was using his beak to drop small amounts of water on the great fire. Tecolotl yelled at Quetzaltotatl to run or fly away to save himself.

Quetzaltotatl responded, "I will not run. I will do the best I can with what I have!" And it is remembered for all time how long ago the forests of the earth were saved from the great fire by a small bird, an owl, and all the people and animals who came together to join them.

What does this story mean to you?

Shine the light

There are many meaningful ways you can help people each day ...

Encouraging:
Helping others by supporting them in achieving their goals.

Praising:
Helping others by recognizing their work, successes, and ideas.

Sharing:
Helping others by sharing with them the abundance in your life.

Giving:
Helping others by giving them your attention, service, or hard work.

Receiving:
Helping others by being grateful and gracious when given something.

Teaching:
Helping others learn important habits, skills, and knowledge.

Listening:
Helping others by paying close attention to what they say and feel.

Volunteering:
Helping others by committing your time and energy to their needs.

Honoring:
Helping others by sincerely reinforcing their perspectives and ideas.

Inspiring:
Helping others believe in themselves and pursue their opportunities.

Healing:
Helping others' body, mind, or spirit heal from pain and suffering.

Loving:
Helping others by loving them for who they are as human beings.

Have you heard?

"To the world you may be one person, but to one person you may be the world." Bill Wilson ~American pioneer in step-based spiritual wellness programs

What do you think he meant by this in terms of helping others?

Did you know?

Life is a process of self-discovery.

Life is a process of self-acceptance.

Life is a process of self-improvement.

And did you know?

We often get confused about the meaning of success.

Success in life can be about an individual achievement.

But it is most meaningful when it involves helping others.

Think about what these principles mean. How might they help you walk your path?

Have you heard?

"It's not how much we accomplish in life but how we treat others along the way that counts. We can get done everything we need to while being kind to other people." Karen Casey ~American spiritual wisdom teacher and writer

"Human greatness does not lie in wealth or power, but in character and goodness." Anne Frank ~German-born diarist and victim of the Holocaust

What do you think they meant?

Haiku for you

This rich daily life

Lighting the path for others

Opens my own heart

Think about this

We can be thoughtful in our beliefs about success. Many people strive to be the best or have the most. We are imprinted by a society of competition, comparison, and a mindset of winning and losing.

It is true that we can win at something as an individual or as part of a team like a soccer game, science fair, or gaming competition. A desire to excel and be the best at a moment in time helps us stretch ourselves.

Trying to be number one all the time, or having the most of something, is a lonely and exhausting path. We can do our best at whatever we are doing but also change our ideas about win and lose, gain and loss.

There is a saying: **Fill life with experiences, not things. Have stories to tell, not stuff to show**.

One way to think about success is that it is the mastery of a skill or talent that is developed over time. What if success is about doing one great thing, not about trying to do everything great?

Success often requires a single mission. Effective people are focused and productive instead of just being busy. They think big, aim high, and act bold, but do the small things each day to achieve their goals.

There is another saying: **People don't fail, they just stop. Success is about not giving up. Never give up**.

What if the reason we feel unsuccessful sometimes is not because we fail but because we give up too soon? We have the courage and strength to keep trying and persist in anything if we set our minds to it.

What if we thought about success in another way? What if we thought about each day as an opportunity to learn and be better than we were the day before? What if success was being more fulfilled and less busy?

What if success in life has to do with being healthy, happy, and helpful? We can avoid the anxiety of competing and comparing, and pursue what is truly meaningful. What if your rubric for success was:

The quality of your friendships …

The various kinds of experiences you have …

The difference you make in the lives of other people …

The mastery of a skill or talent you are very passionate about …

Around the world

Ikigai

(pronounced *icky-guy*)

Ikigai is a Japanese concept that means reason for being or the one thing that makes life worthwhile or why one wakes up in the morning. It is also translated as the happiness and satisfaction one gets from doing an activity he is good at and that holds great meaning.

Ikigai combines ideas of purpose, passion, and meaning. It is a consistent state of being and doing where one achieves her mission daily, almost effortlessly, by doing what she loves to do in both her work and life. Ikigai has been proven to lead to a long fulfilling life.

Did you know?

The natural movement of life can seem dark at times.

We can despair and become cynical about things.

Fate might feel more powerful than faith.

And did you know?

Life is a state of mind — of being and flowing.

We can navigate the flow of life with optimism.

A positive attitude is power to create the life we want.

Think about what these principles mean. How might they help you walk your path?

Have you heard?

"When you arise in the morning, think of what a privilege it is to be alive, to breathe, to think, to enjoy, to love." Marcus Aurelius ~Roman Emperor and Stoic philosopher

What do you think he meant?

Shine the light

As an "A" player on your path, play your "A" game through ...

Awareness:
Are you alert to what is going on in the world and in your mind?

Appreciation:
Are you sincerely grateful for who you are and what you have?

Amazement:
Are you in awe of how extraordinary and sacred life is?

Attitude:
Are you convinced you have the power to decide your state of mind?

Attention:
Are you focused on this present moment right here and right now?

Authenticity:
Are you comfortable just being who you truly are?

Affirmation:
Are you ready to believe that you can achieve whatever you wish?

Adventure:
Are you excited about the possibility that comes with each day?

Have you heard?

"Adventure is worthwhile in itself." Amelia Earhart ~Pioneering American aviator, writer, and equal rights activist

"I don't want an uneventful, safe life. I prefer an adventurous one." Isabel Allende ~Chilean writer, journalist, and activist

What do you think they meant?·

Think about this

Growing up is a process that never ends! It is a lifelong experience in becoming the person we are capable of being. We are always learning about ourselves and learning how to relate to others. Life is a daily adventure in discovery. Each morning is an opportunity to open our hearts and minds to whatever comes our way.

Have you tried treating each day as an adventure?

Check your reality

Have you ever wondered about what you really have control over?

Most of us act as if we have control over our lives. The truth is, while we have some influence, we can't really control much of anything, especially other people. We can't even control our own thoughts and feelings, which is okay! However, there are three things we can totally control: awareness, attention, and attitude.

We have total control, or power, over: our *awareness* of what is going on around us; our *attention* to what we are doing right here and now, without being distracted; and our *attitude*, our state of mind and ability to think and act with positive energy. The belief we can fully control anything else is a story our mind tells us.

What do you think? How might you be more intentional about these three things?

Do you understand?

Once there was an adventurer exploring a dark and dense forest. She had recruited several people from a nearby village, called sherpas, or guides, to carry her equipment and make sure she did not get lost.

The adventurer was always in a hurry. She raced through the forest, already thinking about the next step on her quest, which was to explore and climb the mountain on the other side of the woodland.

After days of rushing through the woods, the sherpas stopped, sat down, and would not go further. She urged them on since she wanted desperately to see everything quickly and then get to the mountain.

They would not move. No matter what she said, they refused. Finally, one of the sherpas admitted why they stopped. He said, "We've moved too fast to get here; now we must wait for our spirits to catch up."

What does this story mean to you? What do you think the sherpa meant?

Have you heard?

"Smile, breathe, and go slowly." Thich Nhat Hanh ~Vietnamese spiritual leader and Buddhist monk

What do you think he meant? Why is it important to slow down your life?

Have you heard?

"Do not ask me where I am going in this limitless world where every step I take is my home." Dōgen ~Japanese Buddhist priest, poet, and founder of the Soto school of Zen

"There are only two paths: the path of awareness and the path of unawareness." Anam Thubten ~Tibetan Buddhist, spiritual leader, writer, and teacher

What do you think they meant?

Do you understand?

Ancient wisdom teachings often come in the form of mind-bending proverbs. Here are a few from different times, sources, and places:

There are many paths to the one truth. Vedas proverb

Ponder the path of your feet and be steadfast in your ways. Christian proverb

Go, not knowing where. Bring, not knowing what. The path is long, the way unknown. Russian proverb

Obstacles do not block the path; they are the path. Zen proverb

A good traveler has no fixed plans and is not intent on arrival. Taoist proverb

Be not afraid of going slowly; be only afraid of standing still. Chinese proverb

To get lost is to learn the way. African proverb

Think about what each of these proverbs mean to you. What are the ways in which these proverbs are related? Is there a main theme?

Shine the light

There is power in positive affirmations that are easy to remember. Here are a few good slogans:

Open your mind

Live to learn

Have no fear

Go with the flow

Keep it simple

Do the right thing

You are worthy

We are one

Be here right now

Which ones do you like? Why do you think slogans are useful? What other wisdom slogans can you come up with?

Have you heard?

"Slogans can become like our breath, our eyesight, our first thought."
Pema Chödrön ~American spiritual teacher, writer, and Buddhist nun

What do you think she meant?

Do you understand?

A brother and sister were snooping in their grandparents' study full of old books and maps and treasures from travels around the world. They found four notecards in a hidden drawer of a mahogany desk.

The first card said *Pursue a career you are passionate about.* The second card said *Commit to lifelong learning.* The third card said *Seek the truth with courage.* And the fourth said *Treat everyone with kindness.*

Then their grandmother suddenly appeared, surprising them. She said, "There you are! Very good, you've been exploring. What did you find? We have learned much in our many adventures, don't you think?"

What do you think? Can a lifetime of discovery be captured on three small notecards?

Have you heard?

"Waking up to who you really are requires letting go of who you imagine yourself to be." Alan Watts ~British philosopher and Zen spiritual wisdom teacher

"The privilege of a lifetime is to become who you really are." Carl Jung ~Swiss psychotherapist and pioneer in psychology

"Knowing yourself is the beginning of all wisdom." Aristotle ~Greek philosopher, scientist, and teacher

What do you think they meant? What do these ideas have in common?

Shine the light

Lao-Tzu was a Chinese philosopher, founder of Taoism, and author of *Tao Te Ching*, which means *the book of the way of virtue*.

Excerpts from two verses in the book adapted by William Martin are:

Wanting more and more, and fearing more and more,
Form the chains that hold us prisoner.

No longer striving to be the people we are supposed to be,
We will find at last that we are free.

How do *want* and *fear* hold us prisoner? When have you felt that you were trying to be someone you are not? What is he saying about true freedom?

Think about this

For millennia philosophers, scholars, and theologians have debated this question: Does essence precede existence, or does existence precede essence? Which comes first, our essence (our true divine nature) or our existence (our life experiences that create our essence)?

In other words, is life an exercise in awakening to who we already are, or is it an exercise in realizing who we can become? **Is life an activity of** *being* **or of** *becoming***?** And what does that mean, if anything, for our freedom, and the personal responsibility that comes with it?

There are other tricky questions in this debate: What is freedom? What does it mean to be free as a conscious being? How are we conditioned by society? How is our freedom compromised? How do we make sense of the world and our life? How can we live authentically?

Which raises another set of questions! What is it to be authentic? What does it mean to live an uncompromising life? How can we think for ourselves and resist just following the herd? **The big challenge before us, then, is to either be, or** *become***, our true selves** *fearlessly.*

What do you think? Is one view better than the other? Can both be true? Why is this such an important question to think about?

Have you heard?

"We don't know what we want and yet we are responsible for what we are." Jean-Paul Sartre ~French Existentialist philosopher and writer

"The mystery of human existence lies not in just living, but in finding something to live for." Fyodor Dostoyevsky ~Russian novelist, journalist, and philosopher

"The only person you are destined to become is the person you decide to be." Ralph Waldo Emerson ~American essayist, poet, and transcendentalist

What do you think they meant?

Epigram I am

In becoming what I want to be,

I think I'm being who I already am!

Pathways

Part 7

Topics

Virtues and values ~ Consciousness

Universal laws ~ True nature and true self

Shine the light

Remember there are universal values and virtues that can guide you on your amazing life journey:

Honesty

Curiosity

Open-mindedness

Compassion

Courage

Humility

Equality

Loving-kindness

Awareness

Positive attitude

Patience

Creativity

Determination

Resilience

Gratitude

Simplicity

Discernment

Dignity

What are your values? Are they consistent with these? What values do you want to learn more about? What values do you want to further develop?

Have you heard?

"Live your life, live it right, be different, do different things." Kendrick Lamar ~African-American hip-hop artist and poet

"Be yourself, everyone else is already taken." Oscar Wilde ~Irish poet, playwright, novelist, and aesthetic

What do you think they meant?

Check your reality

Have you wondered how we can understand reality when our mind does not always perceive reality accurately?

Remember we are not our mind, and that our mind does not always serve us well. We can observe our mind and the common mistakes of perception that prevent us from seeing the world clearly. Here are the most important keys to understanding our mind and reality:

We are not the voice in our head. We do not have to believe that voice. We do not have to do what our mind tells us to do.

We can't control events, but we can control our perception of them. We do not react to an event; we react to our perception of the event.

We may believe that others see the world the same way we do, but they do not. They have their own unique perceptions.

We are often convinced that material things or other people outside of ourselves make us happy. But happiness comes from within.

We often treat our feelings as facts. They are not facts; they are just feelings. We don't have to believe them or be controlled by them.

The most important thing to understand is that we are more alike than we are different, but our mind tells us we are more different than we are alike. We imprison ourselves by perceiving we are separate. We free ourselves by realizing we are all part of the same whole.

Which of these are easy or hard to grasp? How might they help you on your path?

Do you understand?[10]

A young man and his teacher were playing chess. The young man was learning how to play and was beginning to understand the difficulty of the game. He asked, "Master, what is the best move in the world?" The teacher had always thought chess was a lot like life, so he seized on the opportunity to share some wisdom about life and meaning.

The master said, "There is no single best move you can make, just like there is no single meaning of life. Our responsibility is to make the best move we can make in each situation and to find meaning in each moment's experience. Life can be very hard, but we can always realize meaning through our awareness, attention, and attitude."

What do you think? How important is *meaning* in life to you?

Think about this

Your life is speaking to you. Are you listening? The world is sending signals. Are you seeing? The path is teaching you. Are you learning?

Your thoughts are having one wild non-stop party. How positive is your inner conversation? Are you pausing before acting?

There is a reason for everything that happens in your life. What is your responsibility in all of it? Are you aware of your incredible potential?

Whether you know it or not, your life is going in some direction. Are you willing to ask the questions you need for guidance?

There are energy sinks and sources along the way. Are you seeking approval and praise? Or are you forming your own values and beliefs?

There is a quality to your experience so far. What do you want for the future? What is important to you? What are your beliefs and values?

Have you heard?

"Talk to yourself like you would to someone you love." Brené Brown ~American wisdom teacher, researcher, author, and speaker

What do you think she meant?

Change your mind

Change your mindset in attaching to identity, possessions, approval.

Stop trying to be a brand, an image, a false identity, or a fake avatar.

Start believing that you are a key to the universe just the way you are.

Shine the light

Remember to practice the five Nons of equanimity.

Non-judgment: Seek to understand rather than to criticize.
Non-personalizing: Don't take what others say or do personally.
Non-resistance: Accept what is before trying to change it or yourself.
Non-reaction: Pause and put space between thought and action.
Non-attachment: Avoid all forms of craving, grasping, and clinging.

What practices can you put in place? What new habits might you develop?

Check your reality

Remember there are five Laws that govern our universe, have never been disproved, and are the cornerstones of our reality:

The Law of Energy

Everything in the universe is made of energy. All matter and non-matter are pure energy. We are all part of a great cosmic energy field.

The Law of Impermanence

Everything in the universe is always changing. Nothing is permanent, except these laws! Nothing stays the same in our dynamic world.

The Law of Relationship

Everything in the universe is relational. Everything is defined relative to something else. We are all interdependent in an interactive world.

The Law of Unity

Everything in the universe is part of a single reality. Nothing is separate from the whole. We are all unified in a cosmic consciousness.

The Law of Time

Everything in the universe exists only right now. Past and future time are not real. Time is just a mental model we use to explain causality.

Is there another fundamental law of the universe: the law of spirit? How would you define it? How would it relate to the other laws?

True nature is

Sit upright comfortably and close your eyes. For five minutes breathe deeply and slowly. Focus just on your breathing. Be very still and enjoy the wonder of being here now.

Now, reflect on some of the teachings in this guide...

You are alive. You are conscious life. You are a miracle of the cosmos, both ordinary and extraordinary at the same time. The meaning of life is to give meaning to your everyday activity. The purpose of life is to express your true self in meaningful ways.

The quality of your life is determined by the health of your mind, body, and spirit. Fulfillment in your life comes from discovering what is possible and connecting in relationship with people and with nature.

The reality of your life is right now. Pay attention. Stay awake! Be grateful for what is and show compassion and kindness to others. Don't fall asleep from the spell of society's conditioning. With freedom and free will comes responsibility. Stay awake and stay young at heart.

You have the power of awareness. Be intentional about what you do. Open your mind to learning. Show up with a great attitude. Make responsible choices. Smile and open your heart to love and laughter.

Every thought, decision, and action you make creates the path. There is no right or wrong and no such thing as a mistake that can alter it. The path just is. Take care in how you light the path. Remember each step is a step into the exciting unknown.

Today, try to remember...

The path is your life. It is the source of wisdom. It is created by fully experiencing each day. Your path is an awakening to the joy of true self in a connected and changing world.

What have you learned about pathways to a life of sound mind, body, and spirit?

Have you heard?

"A journey of a thousand miles must begin with a single step." Lao-Tzu ~Chinese philosopher and father of Taoism

Do you see that every step on your path can be a new beginning?

Did you know?

Your mind is the power source that will light the path.

Your body is the only home where you will always live.

Your spirit is the loving guide that will lead the way.

Are you ready to fully experience your amazing journey?

Have you heard?

"What lies behind you and what lies before you are tiny matters compared to what lies within you." Ralph Waldo Emerson ~American essayist, poet, and transcendentalist

"Go confidently in the direction of your dreams. Live the life you have imagined." Henry David Thoreau ~American essayist, poet, philosopher, and naturalist

Do you believe you can live the life you imagine?

Haiku for you

The doors are open

Infinite paths welcome me

In lush realms of light

Light your path

Try saying this whenever you need a lift:

I am not my thoughts or my feelings.

I am not my name, what I look like, or what I have.

I am not what people say about me.

I am not my latest test score or my report card.

When I make a mistake, I am not a failure.

I seek to learn from every experience.

I am curious about the world around me.

Wherever I am is where I need to be.

I can feel myself flowing in the river of life.

I can see myself shining like the sun.

I have faith in the goodness of the universe.

My joy comes from inside me.

I like to share this joy with others.

I care about my friends and love my family.

I can change my attitude right now.

I will help another person today.

My spirit is pure, good, and free.

This is who I am.

Light your path

Try saying this when you want to prepare for your day:

I am here and awake right now.

I observe my thoughts and do not judge them.

I do not judge others either.

I do not attach myself to people, places, or things.

I care about people and like to help them.

I listen to others and am open to their views.

I am kind and compassionate.

I tell the truth and speak with care.

I act with integrity and build lasting friendships.

I do not fear the unknown.

I am very comfortable with uncertainty.

I do not dwell on the past.

I do not worry about the future.

I pause, take it easy, and let things go.

I open my heart to the wonder of this life.

I feel gratitude for what I have.

I am thankful for who I am.

I know each day is a new beginning.

I light my path with a smile.

Pathways

Notes

Index of Topics

Index of People

Attributions

Several stories, parables, and poems in the text are centuries old with many different versions and require no attribution. Several are given attribution in the text. Several are footnoted and referenced below.

1. Parable is adapted from Melody Beattie, *More Language of Letting Go* (Hazelden Publishing, 2000)

2. Parable is adapted from Ernest Kurtz and Katherine Ketcham, *The Spirituality of Imperfection* (Bantam Books, 1992)

3. Parable is adapted from Anthony de Mello, *Awareness* (Doubleday Image, 1990)

4. Parable is adapted from Anonymous, *Twenty-four Hours a Day for Teens* (Hazelden Publishing, 2004)

5. Parable is adapted from Carl Honoré, *In Praise of Slowing Down* (HarperOne, 2004)

6. Parable is adapted from Ernest Kurtz and Katherine Ketcham, *The Spirituality of Imperfection* (Bantam Books, 1992)

7. Parable is adapted from Pema Chodron, *Taking the Leap* (Shambhala, 2009)

8. Parable is adapted from Ian Baker, *The Heart of the World* (Penguin Books, 2006)

9. Parable is adapted from Margaret Wheatley, *Turning to One Another* (Berrett-Koehler, 2009)

10. Parable is adapted from Victor Frankl, *Man's Search for Meaning* (Beacon Press, 1959 and 2006)

About the Author

Chris Ellis has lived and worked in every region of the country. He serves organizations and communities as a leader, consultant, coach, educator, mentor, tutor, and volunteer. His passion is to help people of all ages develop their inner wisdom for better living and greater meaning. Chris currently resides in Saint Paul, Minnesota, and is the father of two wonderful young adults. He welcomes correspondence and can be reached at: wisdompathways123@gmail.com.

Made in the USA
Columbia, SC
10 April 2019